Praise for
Meet the New You

"With beautiful integrity and an open heart, Elisa Pulliam encourages women to embrace life. The attitude-focused lenses she recommends reveal vibrant color in daily living."

—RACHEL WOJO, author of *One More Step*

"*Meet the New You* is a fresh road map for those who are really ready to carve out a new path for themselves in life. Pulliam holds your hand like a friend would as she walks you through the five key coaching phases that make this approach to real life change, well, real. Her words speak not only encouragement but also awareness and an ability to take action. *Meet the New You* is more than an enjoyable read; it is a transformational coaching experience offering true personal growth to all who enter into its pages."

—TRISH BLACKWELL, Confidence Coach and author
of *Insecurity Detox*

"*Meet the New You* isn't another quick fix or Band-Aid for my struggles. Instead, it's an encouraging challenge to find the roots of what's keeping me from living the life God has designed me for. I love the way Elisa gently gets to the reader's heart— and then walks her through a transformation that results in real, life-giving, and life-improving change."

—MARY CARVER, co-author of *Choose Joy*

"In *Meet the New You*, Elisa Pulliam beautifully crafts an authentic plan for real life transformation. With her conversational, caring tone, Pulliam reassures her readers that change is indeed possible; tackling obstacles is necessary; and by seeking God and his presence throughout this journey, genuine transformation will take place. This twenty-one day journey is a must-read for any woman longing for a fresh start—a do-over—and the spiritual makeover that makes it all possible."

—JENNY LEE SULPIZIO, author of *For the Love of God*
and *Confessions of a Wonder Woman Wannabe*

"Elisa Pulliam is the coach I always wish I had. In her book *Meet the New You*, she uses her signature grace-filled and honest approach to help you uncover the person you were created to be. If you are ready for a change in direction or simply want to refresh your heart, walk through the pages of this book with Elisa. You will be so glad you did."

—STACY THACKER, co-author of *Hope for the Weary Mom*

"In *Meet the New You*, Elisa Pulliam becomes the personal life coach we all wish we could have. With practical daily focus points, she comes alongside us, helping pinpoint the obstacles holding us back and providing the motivation to reach our fullest potential."

—LYNN COWELL, Proverbs 31 Ministries national speaker
and author of *Magnetic: Becoming the Girl He Wants*

Meet the New You

Meet the New You

A 21-Day Plan for Embracing
Fresh Attitudes and Focused Habits
for Real Life Change

ELISA PULLIAM

Life Coach and Mentor

WATERBROOK
PRESS

Meet the New You
Published by WaterBrook Press
12265 Oracle Boulevard, Suite 200
Colorado Springs, Colorado 80921

All Scripture quotations, unless otherwise indicated, are taken from the Holy Bible, New International Version®, NIV®. Copyright © 1973, 1978, 1984, 2011 by Biblica Inc.™ Used by permission. All rights reserved worldwide. Scripture quotations marked (TLB) are taken from The Living Bible, copyright © 1971. Used by permission of Tyndale House Publishers Inc., Wheaton, Illinois 60189. All rights reserved. Scripture quotations marked (MSG) are taken from The Message by Eugene H. Peterson. Copyright © 1993, 1994, 1995, 1996, 2000, 2001, 2002. Used by permission of NavPress Publishing Group. All rights reserved. Scripture quotations marked (NKJV) are taken from the New King James Version®. Copyright © 1982 by Thomas Nelson Inc. Used by permission. All rights reserved. Scripture quotations marked (NLT) are taken from the Holy Bible, New Living Translation, copyright © 1996, 2004, 2007, 2013. Used by permission of Tyndale House Publishers Inc., Carol Stream, Illinois 60188. All rights reserved.

Details in some anecdotes and stories have been changed to protect the identities of the persons involved.

Trade Paperback ISBN 978-1-60142-794-6
eBook ISBN 978-1-60142-795-3

Copyright © 2015 by Elisa Pulliam

Cover design by Kelly L. Howard

Published in the United States by WaterBrook Multnomah, an imprint of the Crown Publishing Group, a division of Penguin Random House LLC, New York.

WaterBrook® and its deer colophon are registered trademarks of Penguin Random House LLC.

Library of Congress Cataloging-in-Publication Data
Pulliam, Elisa.
   Meet the new you : a 21-day plan for embracing fresh attitudes and focused habits for real life change / Elisa Pulliam. — First Edition.
      pages cm
   Includes bibliographical references.
      ISBN 978-1-60142-794-6 — ISBN 978-1-60142-795-3 (electronic) 1. Christian women—Religious life. 2. Self-actualization (Psychology)—Religious aspects—Christianity. 3. Self-actualization (Psychology) in women. I. Title.
   BV4527.P84 2015
   248.8'43—dc23

                              2015024786

Printed in the United States of America
2015—First Edition

10 9 8 7 6 5 4 3 2 1

Special Sales
Most WaterBrook Multnomah books are available at special quantity discounts when purchased in bulk by corporations, organizations, and special-interest groups. Custom imprinting or excerpting can also be done to fit special needs. For information, please e-mail SpecialMarkets@WaterBrookMultnomah.com or call 1-800-603-7051.

Mr. Blue Eyes, you've seen me through the lens of Christ since day one, and you called out the new me before I was even interested in meeting her. Thank you for loving me as Christ loves His bride and turning me toward the fullness of life God offers. I wouldn't have wanted to find the new me with anyone other than you, and I am so grateful for the way this miracle of transformation radically impacts the next generation, especially our children, whom we so deeply love together.

But I wish it to be distinctly understood all through, that, unless I believed with all my heart in God's effectual working on His side, not one word of this book would ever have been written.

—Hannah Whitall Smith,
The Christian's Secret of a Happy Life

Let this be written for a future generation,
    that a people not yet created may praise the Lord.

—Psalm 102:18

Contents

Phase 3: Overcome Obstacles

Phase 4: Stick with Solutions

Phase 5: A Vibrant New Vision

It's Already Begun

He who began a good work in you
will carry it on to completion.

—Philippians 1:6

Right now I'm picturing you skimming through these words wondering, *Is this book for me?*

You're looking for an answer. A solution. Maybe a way out. Possibly a step forward.

The idea of meeting the new you might sound pretty enticing, yet maybe you think real transformation is impossible. It's not as if you can step into a machine, then presto, emerge as a new person. Doesn't real change take time, focus, and concerted effort? Yes. But it doesn't have to be quite so daunting.

Real change happens when you start embracing fresh attitudes and focused habits, all in light of God's grace and truth.

Friend—if I may call you that already—I know authentic life change is possible, not only because of what I've witnessed in the lives of the women I coach, but also because I've lived it myself. Oh, if you had met me twenty years ago, you would have seen a hardhearted, reckless, and destined-for-devastation woman. Trust me when I say I was a train wreck whom God was merciful enough to rescue, using Christ-with-skin-on folks to show me a better way. I can't wait to give you the nitty-gritty of that story later on because, honestly, the core of who I am changed the day I came to believe in Jesus as my Savior.

But hear this too: God's transforming work in me hasn't been a once-and-done experience. It is ongoing as He pours His love and truth into my heart and opens my eyes to see life from His perspective. That's also what I want for you! I want you to experience the presence of God and get to know Him more personally.

> And when God is personally present, a living Spirit, that old, constricting legislation is recognized as obsolete. We're free of it! All of us! Nothing between us and God, our faces shining with the brightness of his face. And so we are transfigured much like the Messiah, our lives gradually becoming brighter and more beautiful as God enters our lives and we become like him. (2 Corinthians 3:17–18, MSG)

Isn't that the heart of real life transformation: to be changed from the inside out by the presence of God at work within us? But it's not only us that He changes. When God gets hold of you and me, He redeems the legacies we inherited and the ones we're passing on. He's turned the legacy I was given—one marred by physical and emotional abuse and all sorts of dysfunction—into a beautiful story depicting His grace, mercy, and redemptive power. In the pages ahead, I'll share how that story has unfolded in the context of what God accomplished in me and through me for His glory as my thinking and habits conformed to the truth found in Scripture.

While I am living life on the other side of being the new me, I'm still seeking God for continuous work in my heart, mind, and soul. Gone is the bitter, cranky, critical, and defensive woman who was always putting on a mask and pursuing perfection. In her place is one who is walking in the grace of God, overflowing with His hope and humbled by His provision. It's amazing how yielding my life to God and giving Him my issues enabled my temper to simmer down and grew my ability to love, laugh, and live life to the fullest. However, that doesn't mean I have it all together. I still battle insecurity and worry. I lose my cool. I veer away from my God-given priorities. There are areas in my life in which I feel stuck. But I'm not who I was, and I have hope of becoming more and more like that woman God intends.

Maybe that's what you desire—simply to become that woman you believe God always intended you to be . . . a woman who is brighter and more beautiful, inside and out. But how do you make that happen?

Maybe you are ready to get out of the cycle of being overwhelmed and worn down, but you don't have the energy required to make progress. Maybe you feel stuck every time you look at your finances or those evil numbers staring back at you from the bathroom scale. But how do you get below the surface to deal with the real issues?

Maybe you have a dream you'd like to begin walking toward, but fear holds you back like an army of giants. Maybe you're simply craving a fresh start as you embrace your new normal, yet you don't know where to begin.

Whatever the reason for wanting to meet the new you, it is entirely valid, my friend. That thing you want to overcome, resolve, or push through may be different from my thing or someone else's (because let's face it, we're always comparing), yet we can lock arms and approach the process of transformation from the same starting point: the truth.

The truth is that you're not stuck permanently. You can change.

Imagine, for a moment, if you declared the end of an era—of being stuck. Maybe it's moving on from that habit of criticism, unforgiveness, and victim mentality. What if you finally pursued your God-given dreams while embracing your current responsibilities? How about if you learned how to carve out margin for rest and fun? What if you accepted your God-given wiring and embraced the life you've been given to live today?

I'm here to encourage you to take that brave next step, prayerfully, carefully, and thoughtfully, toward real life change, whatever that change may look like for you.

It's time to meet the new you through . . .

- uncovering the story God is writing through your life
- discovering your God-given identity and wiring
- facing the obstacles before you through the power of God at work in you
- seeking the Lord for relevant, biblically sound solutions
- carving out a vision for your future based on God's purposes for your life

You might be thinking, *But how can we accomplish all that in a twenty-one-day journey?* Good question! Let me suggest that you consider *Meet the New You* as your starting point. As a store owner might take an inventory of her goods to decide which products to order next, this journey will help you assess what your life looks like today while allowing you to gain clarity and vision about tomorrow. This process works because each chapter has been purposefully and prayerfully put together using life-coaching techniques designed to help women like you, who desire to get unstuck and embrace change.

If this idea of life coaching is new to you, let me explain how it works. A life coach is like an architect who comes alongside clients to help them define what they want to build. In contrast, a counselor is more like an archaeologist who goes in for the dig, seeking to uncover what happened in the past and how that is influencing the present. While a client's whole life story is taken into consideration in the life-coaching process, the focus is on moving forward and strategizing a vision that is fully directed by the client. So, as life coach, I come to you with this mind-set, and as a Christian, I wholly believe that the God of the universe has the answer for you. I don't need to tell you what to do, but rather I get to co-labor with God through asking thought-provoking questions that challenge you to seek His best for your life.

The information I will share with you is a tool I wish I'd had twenty years ago. I've written this book because I'm passionate about authentic life transformation, not only because it's good for me and for you, but especially because of the impact our changed lives will have on the next generation. Every time I look at my family, I'm reminded that the way I live my life is of grave importance, because it is influencing the ones I love most. I think you'll glimpse this in the pages ahead, so I'd like to introduce my brood to you.

Leah, my oldest, is only sixteen, but it seems as though she's already got one foot out the door on the way to the rest of her life, which will likely involve her love of sports and family. Abby, my fourteen-year-old, is our strong leader, paving her way into her future and caring for every soul she meets. Luke, my ten-year-old deep thinker and creative builder, is full of wisdom beyond his years. And Kaitlyn, our bonus baby (yes, Luke's twin), is my big-idea girl who wishes she didn't have to wait to grow up in order to make her brilliant plans—such as owning a horse farm—a reality. Steadying our craziness is my incredibly loyal, totally dependable husband, Stephen, who also happens to be an amazing chemistry teacher (he's great to have around during homework time). He's guaranteed to be pushing from behind whenever I feel like quitting this journey of transformation, and he is really the reason it all began in the first place.

These five remember the old me—that sharp-tongued, fear-driven woman who spent a great deal of time yelling. And every single day they motivate me to keep becoming that woman God intended.

What will be the source of your motivation?

Will it be your children, grandchildren, or spiritual children? Will it be the impact you'll have at work, in your ministry, with your extended family?

This life isn't just about you. It's about God using you in this world for His great and mighty purpose. Yes, you, because you matter that much!

Will you entertain the idea that experiencing real life change might be for the people around you as much as it is for you? Oh friend, God designed your life on purpose and for good purpose. No matter how you feel about yourself today, the truth is that He's not done with what He started on the day you were conceived.

He who began a good work in you will carry it on to completion until the day of Christ Jesus. (Philippians 1:6)

You're not a hopeless case, and you won't be forever stuck. Real change is possible as God continues lifelong transformative work in your heart, mind, body, and soul.

Your heavenly Father longs for you to join Him in His work. He's patiently waiting for you to allow truth to become the foundation for how you live. He wants you to seek Him as you consider His ways afresh so that you can discover how to do life differently than what you have done in the past.

Real life change is a process built on a partnership between you and God.

Will you say yes to this divine invitation? Turn the page, and I'll show you how to begin.

How to Use *Meet the New You*

With each day tackling a different topic, *Meet the New You* is all about encountering God personally as you look at your life from a new perspective. Using the same approach I do with my life-coaching clients, I'll be asking you thought-provoking questions to get you thinking about solutions that are reasonable, biblical, and right for your life today. Each section of the book corresponds to one of the five key phases of coaching:

Phase 1: Awareness

Phase 2: Assessment

Phase 3: Obstacles

Phase 4: Solutions

Phase 5: Vision

These phases are designed to help you get a sense of where you are today and where you want to be in the future while figuring out what is standing in your way. That might sound like a lot to accomplish in one book, but it's a process that you can move through at your own pace. You might even decide to take more than twenty-one days, especially if you choose to take the weekends off. No one is keeping track of how long it takes you, so walk in grace.

In each day's reading, you'll find biblical application, an activity to work through, reflection questions, and a closing Scripture prayer designed to help you find the solutions that fit your life. Make the most of this opportunity by giving yourself evidence of your efforts—something to look back on when you're done. Use a journal or notebook to record your thoughts as you work through the exercises and questions. If you want to dig further into the Scriptures, look up the verses listed at the end of the prayers. You may choose to read the verses in context and record in your journal any portions that stand out. If you choose to embrace this journey with friends or in a group (which would be a great experience and ideal for accountability), the questions lend themselves to group discussion.

Approaching the Process of Change

Did you know that embracing fresh attitudes and focused habits is actually a scientific process and not just a theological undertaking? That's because of *plasticity*, which simply means your brain remembers your actions like pathways, and those pathways can be changed.[1] Isn't that great news? Change is possible—although real change requires real work to carve out those new pathways in your brain. Here is how the process works:

> Imagine there is a field in front of you. To the left is a beaten-down path leading to your neighbor's house, but it winds a couple of miles out of the way. You're tired of the time it takes to go in that direction, so you decide to carve a new path that could take you straight across the field in fewer than fifteen minutes as compared to the usual forty-five.
>
> Grabbing a machete, you get to work. After hours of labor, you see progress, but you've got so much farther to go. The sun is beating down and scorching your back, so you quit for the day with plans to start again tomorrow.
>
> The next morning you wake up with good intentions. However, the sound of raindrops tapping on the roof entices you to stay cozy inside. Days later, the rain hasn't quit. The work you did on the new path feels pointless as you see the new wildflowers sprouting, while the old path is still not yet overgrown. What would you do? Would you quit creating that new path and just use the old one?

It takes as much effort to leave that old path behind as it does to carve out the new one. Why? Because the old one is more comfortable and familiar and requires no work, while the new one demands dedication and focus.

Yes, sticking with old habits is easier than forming new ones.

So what should you do? You have to keep the cost in mind. Staying "as is" will add up over the long haul. Putting in the effort toward change may feel exhausting now, but you will reap so much later on. Plus, there's a secret about change: once you begin to see results, you'll be motivated to keep working toward that goal of real transformation. So how about putting into practice an approach that will enable you to embrace fresh attitudes and focused habits, one thought and one action step at a time? That's where "Trap and Transform" comes in!

The Trap and Transform technique is an approach built from two key principles found in Scripture:

Principle 1: Trap Your Thoughts and Attitudes. We demolish arguments and every pretension that sets itself up against the knowledge of God, and we take captive every thought to make it obedient to Christ. (2 Corinthians 10:5)

Principle 2: Transform Your Habits. Do not conform to the pattern of this world, but be transformed by the renewing of your mind. Then you will be able to test and approve what God's will is—his good, pleasing and perfect will. (Romans 12:2)

The Trap and Transform process is simply an intentional way to consider how your thoughts and attitudes impact the way you're living, especially your habits. It's a concept sown into each chapter, but it's really a process that can mark every single moment for the rest of your life. Picture it this way: Imagine using a butterfly net to catch all your thoughts. With them trapped, take each one before God and consider them in light of the Scriptures. Ask the Lord to help you discern the truth and demolish the lies—so that your habits conform to the way God intends for you to live.

If you are new to this idea of using the Bible as a tool for everyday living, take heart—*Meet the New You* will help you get started with foundational truths and plenty of suggestions on how to grow in your understanding of Scripture. If you've been living a life of faith for some time, this journey will enable you to intentionally consider how your thinking and living line up with God's purposes.

So how about turning the page for a fresh encounter with God so that you can uncover the life He designed you to lead? But before we start, may I ask God to pour out His blessing on you?

Heavenly Father, please enter the heart and mind of this precious woman.
Fill her with Your love and grace. Give her fresh attitudes and focused
habits that are rooted deeply in Your Word. Most of all, give her a vision
to see beyond today and get a glimpse of the woman she is becoming—the
woman who delights in joining You in Your work as she embraces ongoing,
real life change. In Jesus's name, amen.

Phase 1

A Fresh Awareness

Prayerfully consider what's happening in your life right now and then make a commitment to remain consistent in your conversation with and dependence on God. The courage, direction, and divine favor you'll receive from an ongoing fresh relationship with the Savior is exactly what you'll need to stay on track.

—PRISCILLA SHIRER

Zoom Out

Sketch Your Life Map

Where God is making new life, not a day
goes by without his unfolding grace.

—2 Corinthians 4:16, msg

My natural tendency is to look at life from a bird's-eye view, which is probably a by-product of my creative side. I can't think clearly unless I see everything before me, which means you'll often find me making a diagram, fixing a spreadsheet, or creating a list anytime I feel the pressure to make a decision or push through an obstacle.

This big-picture way of thinking is something I learned to do in one of my first college art classes. We were tasked with spending more than two months sketching a curtain that never moved. (So boring!) I balked at the project . . . until the term came to a close and I saw all the skill I had gained. Surprisingly, not only did I learn how to draw, but I also discovered how to look at life differently. By studying the shadows, I began to see the interplay of darkness and light to define shape and depth. I discovered the importance of taking in the whole composition before planning where I should begin the drawing.

That, my friend, is why I think it's so important to step back and to see the big picture when it comes to approaching life change. While focusing on one area is necessary at times, looking at life from a broad perspective is an effective way to identify where to invest time and attention for real life change.

So, what would you think about stepping back to look at your whole life picture? Don't panic! I won't ask you to spend the next two months drawing a self-portrait (or a curtain!). But I will ask you to zoom out to see what's going on in your life before you zoom in. This process is much like what the Bible describes as shifting our focus from the seen to unseen:

> So we fix our eyes not on what is seen, but on what is unseen, since what is
> seen is temporary, but what is unseen is eternal. (2 Corinthians 4:18)

The seen. That's what we humans like to focus on: The laundry piles in the den. The weeds in the garden. The dust on the bookshelf.

What parts of your life are you focusing on? Do you see what's left undone while missing what's accomplished? Or do you focus on what's accomplished and feel guilty about what's left undone?

As you begin to look at every aspect of your life from a fresh perspective, I encourage you to keep this one question in mind: What does God have to say about this?

Depending on what you think of God, that idea might be enticing . . . or a total turnoff. If He's a great big ogre in the sky who sends curses your way, you may not be inclined to see things from His perspective. I get that. I have not always seen the goodness of God—in fact, I still remember the days when I was afraid of ending up on His bad side. But the truth is that God doesn't operate this way. He is loving, kind, faithful, and merciful, just as the Bible describes (Psalm 100:5; 103:8; 145:17). He longs to meet our needs and pour His grace upon us. The Lord is on our side. He doesn't want us to give up and settle on life "as is," no matter how hard it seems at the moment. He's got a bigger plan at work that He wants us to set our sights upon:

> So we're not giving up. How could we! Even though on the outside it often
> looks like things are falling apart on us, on the inside, where God is making
> new life, not a day goes by without his unfolding grace. These hard times
> are small potatoes compared to the coming good times, the lavish celebra-
> tion prepared for us. There's far more here than meets the eye. The things
> we see now are here today, gone tomorrow. But the things we can't see now
> will last forever. (2 Corinthians 4:16–18, MSG)

"These hard times are small potatoes compared to the coming good times." I love that. God's grace is weaving its way into every detail of your life, even the parts that may seem overlooked, such as being passed over for a job promotion, having an offer on a house fall through, suffering through a difficult relationship, navigating singleness, hitting obstacles while trying to launch a ministry, or struggling to get a company off the ground.

No matter your situation, His grace is there.

That's the unseen truth. That's what I want you to start looking for as you shift your perspective from the earthly to the eternal. Friend, this planet is not your final destination—it's simply the rest stop on the way to one that is far more magnificent, where a "lavish celebration" is being prepared for you. But while you wait to meet Jesus face to face, God has business for you to accomplish. The challenges you're facing in your external life are designed to reshape your intentions to be more like His (2 Corinthians 3:16–18, MSG).

So how about bucking your human nature, which tends to focus on only what is seen, and beginning to look at life from a brand-new perspective? We'll start by getting your life down on paper before going deeper to see what's happening beneath the surface.

Trap and Transform

Map Your Life

What would you think about starting this journey at one of my favorite places? While a real-life tour of the Metropolitan Museum of Art (the Met) would be absolutely fabulous, in the interest of time and money, let's head over to the Met's website and look at a beautiful Vincent van Gogh painting. If you've got your computer or smartphone handy, go to http://bit.ly/1Gn2IML.

If you visited the Met in person, you might have to push through the crowds to get a good look at Van Gogh's *Sunflowers.* Maybe you'd find a spot on a bench where you could linger and study the whole painting. Your perspective will shift as you select the position from which you choose to focus. Try this out by clicking on the painting. A new window will open, and you'll see Plus and Minus buttons. Click on these to zoom in or out. If you view the painting up close, it looks like smudges of paint. Only when you zoom out can you discover the beauty of the whole composition: the sunflowers with that calming blue background.

This is exactly the process we go through when it comes to focusing on our lives. The problem is that we usually get stuck on the Zoom-In button and obsess over a problem. Oftentimes we can find the solution when we zoom out to get the big-picture perspective . . . which is God's perspective.

God is the master Artist painting the picture of your life, and He sees the whole canvas.

The smudge of color that looks like a mistake may very well become the focal point of the composition as God works it into His perfect creation. Your vantage point determines your perspective, which is why creating a life map is so helpful. By zooming out, you'll see the pieces of your life with new clarity as you make strides toward balance and purpose.

Sketch Your Life Map

Are you relieved that you don't need any artistic talent to accomplish this assignment? All you have to do is draw boxes and lines. So go grab a pencil and a blank sheet of paper, then sketch out the diagram below. Personalize your diagram by adding additional boxes for every aspect of your life. For example, you might have a line pointing to the left of the *Work and Life Chores* box for

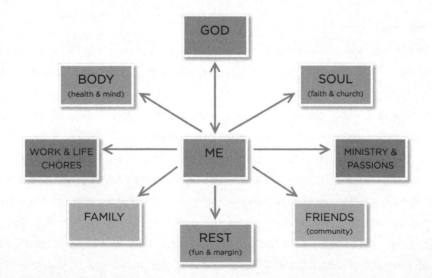

each of the following: volunteering, cleaning the house, shopping, paying bills—you get the idea. The goal is to get all your relationships and responsibilities listed on this one diagram.

Once you look at your life map, you might think, *Now that I see it all, I'm totally overwhelmed.* That's okay! Chances are you're so busy that you didn't have a clear sense of what was filling up your time. Maybe you see what needs to change and are eager to get started. Or maybe you discover there are important parts missing from your map. That's okay too.

You're only sketching your life, remember, not casting it in stone.

No matter how you feel about your life map, I encourage you to spend time talking to God about what you see and ask Him to give you the courage to face reality as you remember the gift of His unfolding grace. Don't rush forward, attempting overnight change; instead, camp out in this necessary phase of gaining awareness before moving toward real life change.

Go Deeper

1. How would you like your life map to look different a year from now? Take time to talk with God about your dreams and desires while asking Him to line them up with His.

2. As you think about the process of change as it relates to your life map, how do you feel? Excited, afraid, overwhelmed?

3. Having zoomed out to create your life map, what issues or obstacles do
   you see? List your circumstances, relationships (use initials to keep this
   confidential), responsibilities, emotional or spiritual issues, physical
   challenges, and so on, and ask God for His perspective going forward.

Give It Over

*Heavenly Father, I want to become a woman who is passionate about
the process of transformation. Show me how to cooperate with You
to see Your purposes accomplished in my life. Give me the courage to
consider life from a fresh perspective as I welcome Your unfolding grace.
In Jesus's name, amen. (2 Corinthians 4:16–18, MSG)*

The Days of Our Lives

What Fills Your Time

Make the most of every opportunity.

—COLOSSIANS 4:5, MSG

What do you think is your number one time consumer in an average week? Is it in caring for the littles or playing chauffeur for the preteens? Is it being distracted by social media or doing your best to keep up with the chores? Is it work (and what comes home with you), running a ministry, or caring for aging parents?

Time is consumed, with or without your permission.

Your hours will be devoted to someone and something, so how do you know what should get first dibs? How can you make sure you're using your day the best way possible? Well, what if you looked at your time according to your intentional priorities and sense of God's purposes for your life? Moreover, what if you looked at time as though it didn't really belong to you in the first place?

The fact is, time doesn't belong to us. It's God's clock we're punching! He spun this world into being, set the week in motion, and already numbered all of our days (Genesis 1; Job 14:5; Psalm 90:12). He knew us from the point of our conception—long before we knew ourselves! He knows even our final breath (Psalm 139). God understands time in a way we'll never comprehend, so what if we took our cues from Him on how to work within its limitations?

To begin with, God wants us to make the most of our time:

Don't waste your time on useless work, mere busywork, the barren pursuits of darkness. . . . So watch your step. Use your head. Make the most of every chance you get. These are desperate times! (Ephesians 5:11–16, MSG)

Our days are His. Our hours are His. Our minutes are His. And He has a purpose for every one of them.

So instead of seeing time as something that consumes us, let's view it as a tool we get to use. Let's see time as simply the framework for the story that God is unfolding in our lives.

Time will pass between your fingers and weave around every breath. You can't stop it, grab it, or bottle it. But you can live purposefully in it.

Imagine if you looked at what fills your day in light of what God might want to accomplish through you. Rather than focusing solely on your to-do list and material comforts, reflect on how a God-influenced perspective would impact the way you use your time.

ONE LITTLE TWEAK

Early in my life-coaching career, I offered to practice my new skills with my friend Lauren. She was itching for a change in her life because time seemed to be slipping away without her permission. She was still reeling from her family's cross-country move three years earlier, which impacted her career, her community, and how she used her time. Yes, *time.*

Back on the West Coast, Lauren had balanced an active professional life as a singer with being a mom and wife. When they moved, she and her husband decided that she'd let go of her career to focus on her family's needs as they adjusted to living in a new place. Well, her family was finally settled, but Lauren was not. Her days seemed wasted, even though she valued caring for her family and connecting with her new community.

After I asked Lauren to describe her life, it became clear that there was a twofold problem: one, she felt aimless without her career because music was also her passion (what God wired her to do); and two, she had no idea how to find time to begin rebuilding her passion and possibly a future career. So we did a time-evaluation exercise. I gave Lauren a blank worksheet and asked her to fill it in over the course of a week, recording every commitment and activity each day. A week later, we pored over her results and discovered that if she went grocery shopping during her son's karate lesson, she'd gain an hour a week to devote to her singing. As Lauren looked at how that one small change brought her the gift of time, she began to consider other ways to create a more efficient routine. Within months, those extra few hours each week led to opportunities to sing at some rather prestigious venues. Although Lauren didn't relaunch her full-time career, she found enough passion-refueling to bring a sense of satisfaction back into her life.

Just a little tweak in how Lauren used her time to act on her God-given passion and priorities changed her overall sense of life purpose. Can you imagine how this could happen in your life too?

Trap and Transform

Evaluate Your Time

Maybe, like my friend Lauren, you need to make one little tweak in your schedule to better use the time God has given you. Or maybe you already know which commitment needs to end so you can escape being always behind, never on time. Maybe the way you use your time feels just fine, but you've never actually consulted God about it. By utilizing the time-evaluation worksheet, you can get an honest pulse on how you spend your days. The goal isn't to harshly judge what you're doing but rather to take stock so you can make wise decisions about how to live differently going forward.

Step 1: Record Your Reality

Create a time-evaluation worksheet: a spreadsheet with days of the week across the top and your waking hours (in half-hour blocks) down the side. For your convenience, I have a template you can download at http://bit.ly/1KJK9eI. Record how you spend your time over the next three to seven days.

Step 2: Sketch Your Ideal Schedule

Print out a second time-evaluation worksheet in order to pencil out what your ideal schedule or routine would look like. Essentially, this is how you would spend your time if everything in your day went according to plan. Once you have it figured out, tuck it away for reference later on. Don't try to live by it—unless all you have to do is make a minor tweak here or there. When it comes time to build your real schedule, your ideal plan will come into play.

Go Deeper

1. What is your number one time consumer? Does it reflect a deliberate choice, or would you like it to change?

2. Could you be making better use of your time? If so, explain your thoughts.

3. Can you envision how a small change in your schedule might allow you to explore your passions while still focusing on your responsibilities? What steps can you take to move in this direction?

Give It Over

Heavenly Father, thank You for the reminder that I need to be inten-
tional about making the most of every opportunity. Lord, I know this
is hard to do, especially when distractions compete with the people
who really need my attention and the tasks that are mine to accomplish.
Help me to be wise, Lord, in how I steward this time You have given me.
In Jesus's name, amen. (Colossians 4:13, MSG)

Whatever You Do

Order Your Priorities

Whatever you do, work at it with all
your heart, as working for the Lord.

—Colossians 3:23

Now that you're thinking about how to use your time, let's take it one step further by focusing on how to prioritize your relationships, responsibilities, and resources. These priorities will ultimately help you determine a fresh new routine and shape how you spend your time in the future.

Let me illustrate how this works: Imagine having an empty jar that you need to fill with a combination of rocks, pebbles, and sand. All of them are designed to fit in the jar, but you must load them in the proper order or they all won't all fit. Do you know what you should put in first? The rocks, because they take up the most space, followed by the pebbles, which will fall into the empty spaces, before you finally put in the sand, which will slide into the crevices.

My friend, your life is like a jar. Only so much can fit into it, so you need to identify the rocks, pebbles, and sand and put them in the jar in the right order. This has been a struggle for me because I always think my jar is bigger than it is. However, as I've worked toward practicing what I preach, I've been able to parse out my priorities in a way that finally makes sense. The big rocks are my relationship with God, my husband and children, and family and friends as well as embracing opportunities to share the gospel and God's love with others. The pebbles pertain to details: caring for my home, work, other ministry responsibilities, and taking care of my health. And the sand, well, that's the laundry, chores, and challenges I'd rather ignore but must fit into my life.

While my priorities may not reflect yours, identifying them has given me freedom to allow baskets of clean laundry to sit in the den, like jets lined up on the tarmac, without a shred of guilt. And that, my friend, is a miracle.

You see, for too many years, I thought I was a failure as a housekeeper because I couldn't stay on top of the laundry folding. No matter how well I stuck to my routine of tossing a new load into the washer each morning and making sure it hit the dryer cycle by dinnertime, inevitably I left those freshly dried clothes abandoned for days on end. I finally let go of the guilt when I accepted that the reason wasn't my lack of ability but rather my priorities—an intentional choice. I *chose* to spend more time on other things because I believed that having clean laundry was just as good as having *folded* clean laundry . . . and the unfolded loads could wait there for a while without hurting anyone. I accepted that folding laundry was sand and not rocks in my jar. Mind you, it's still a responsibility that I will get to, but it's not the priority I had once thought it needed to be. Depending upon the chaos of the week, and the unexpected crisis of the day, I might let the laundry go, allow the dishes to pile up in my sink, and put off scrubbing the tub until it's absolutely necessary. I have decided that those are the tasks that can wait, as least for a few hours or more, while I work on something that's more important.

Which of your responsibilities is a source of guilt or condemnation? Could that guilt be misplaced? Or is it time to shake up your priorities?

The truth is that we all have something, or someone, waiting on us.

Maybe it's the pile of junk mail taking up priceless real estate on the kitchen counter. Or the school paperwork waiting to be read, signed, and returned. Or a boss who wants the project summary turned in yesterday.

At the heart of the matter, the issue is not what's waiting, but why it's waiting.

Ironically, in life coaching, we're never supposed to ask why because it automatically puts a person on the defensive. If I came right out and asked, "Why haven't you done _____?," you might feel as though I'd overstepped a few boundaries. So let me pose the question in a different way: *Is there something or someone waiting on you because you're avoiding your responsibilities?*

If you search for the answer to that question, you'll uncover your priorities and begin to see the core thinking that's influencing your daily habits.

It's Really a Heart Thing

When we consider what's been left undone in a day, we need to figure out if we're being neglectful or intentional. In other words, are we pursuing the opportunities God is laying before us—or running from them? Are we embracing the work He has for us or rejecting it? Yes, *work*. See, God has designed us to work, which is about so much more than simply what we get paid to do. All of our responsibilities, whether folding laundry, reading to a child, running a ministry, or attending a business meeting, are work in God's eyes. Our work is what we put our hands to— the tasks we love and hate, the ones we've chosen, and the ones we can't get out of doing.

This work matters much to God, regardless of how the world perceives or receives it.

Your work is significant not because of the outcome but because of the motive— meaning the state of your heart—whether you're washing one more dish, completing one more spreadsheet, or matching one more pair of socks.

> Whatever you do, work at it with all your heart, as working for the Lord,
> not for human masters, since you know that you will receive an inher-
> itance from the Lord as a reward. It is the Lord Christ you are serving.
> (Colossians 3:23–24)

Would you agree that if all of your work is to be done for the glory of God, then anyone else for whom you do it matters a lot less?

Your work is holy when you're doing it for the glory of God.

Those very people you devote your time to serving—whether family, friends, colleagues, or strangers—move into a priority position in your life, not because they deserve it, but because you see them through the lens of God's love and His desires for their eternal good. This shift in thinking considers time and work under God's sovereign purposes rather than our willy-nilly wishes, which is exactly what Henry and Richard Blackaby write about in *Experiencing God.* They suggest that we shift our focus so that we can "watch to see where God is working and join Him!"[2] What a liberating way of living!

After more than a decade of living this way, I can promise that God will open your eyes to see His work simply because you ask Him. You'll also discover that your work won't look like anyone else's. Can you imagine how that could relieve the guilt you live with all too often?

God's glorious work is set apart for you and me.

His work. His timing. His purposes. God wants to establish all of your work according to how He made you. So imagine if when your feet hit the floor in the morning, you said to God, *Show me Your work today, Lord. I want to join You in it!* Imagine waking up to God's fresh new mercies and asking Him how you should tend to your responsibilities, relationships, and resources, because you trust His holy purposes, even when the tasks may be as mundane as laundry folding, tub scrubbing, or setting a meeting agenda with a new client.

The mundane will become holy when it's done for the glory of God.

So let's consider how you can approach your work according to God-ordered priorities.

Trap and Transform

Order Your Priorities

Have you ever taken an inventory on how you're spending your time, not in terms of schedule but by prioritizing your tasks? This can be such an eye-opening exercise as you look closely at the *why* behind the *what* of your responsibilities, relationships, and resources while also setting forth new priorities that will lead to lasting change. Be encouraged that this process will get easier and feel more natural over time, especially as you make this evaluation exercise a regular habit.

Step 1: Consider Your Responsibilities

Using your life map and time-evaluation worksheet, list the jobs, chores, and details you have to accomplish in a given day, week, and month. Be sure to

include caring for your spiritual, physical, and emotional health. (You'll probably need more lines than those here.) Next to the responsibility, indicate the
priority number: Priority 1 = Must happen; Priority 2 = Important; Priority 3 =
Not important; Priority 4 = Can be eliminated.

Responsibility	Priority #

Step 2: Consider Your Relationships

Looking at your life map and time-evaluation worksheet, make a list of people with whom you share a relationship—spouse and children, extended family, friends, and colleagues or coworkers. Then rank what you believe should be their priority in your life in terms of how frequently they need your time and attention: Priority 1 = Daily; Priority 2 = Weekly; Priority 3 = Monthly; Priority 4 = Rarely.

Relationship	Priority #

Step 3: Consider Your Resources

How are you stewarding your resources? In the same way time is a resource to be ordered, your financial resources (what you own and the money you have) should also be used in light of your God-given priorities. For example, while it's necessary to spend money on mortgage or rent, utilities, groceries, clothing, entertainment, gifts, and so on, are you spending the appropriate amounts in these areas? Are you being excessive or being stingy? Are your gifts to others extravagant when something more modest would suffice? Conversely, could you shift some personal eating-out budget to treat a friend to lunch or bless someone having a hard time with flowers and a card? Is your home a gathering place or just storing up stuff? Could you use your community clubhouse to host a Bible study? If you have a boat, can you invite people out on the water with you, or is it only for your pleasure?

Using the space provided (and more if needed), make a list of all your resources, such as your savings account, home or property, luxury toys (such as a boat or motor home), tools (such as a snow blower or woodworking equipment), home and hobby items (such as a sewing machine), and indicate how you feel God may want you to use those resources to benefit others as you seek to be eternally-minded.

Resource	How to Use It

Resource	How to Use It

If you'd like to take this concept of being intentional about your financial resources to the next level, I highly recommend Dave Ramsey's Financial Peace University.[3] He'll teach you everything you need to know about managing your finances well and provide a step-by-step guide for getting out of debt.

Go Deeper

1. How does thinking about your work in terms of how to best use the hours God has given you change your perspective about your responsibilities, relationships, and resources?

2. Which area of your life—responsibilities, relationships, or resources—do you feel needs the most attention right now?

3. What steps should you take to prioritize joining God in His work rather than asking Him to join you in yours?

Give It Over

Heavenly Father, thank You for establishing the work of my hands. Help me to be disciplined about surrendering my will to Your plans and working for Your glory. Show me how to consider my priorities with the mind-set of serving You above all else. In Jesus's name, amen. (Psalm 90:17; Colossians 3:23–24)

Mind the Gap, Please

Look at Your Story Time Line

Your very lives are a letter that anyone
can read by just looking at you.

—2 CORINTHIANS 3:3, MSG

One of my favorite life-coaching concepts is the idea of *minding the gap*. When I hear that phrase, I can't help but pretend I'm back in London during my junior year in college riding the Tube. Every time those train doors opened, the conductor would graciously encourage riders to "Mind the gap, please"—meaning, "Pay attention to the space between the train and platform."

Today is all about minding the gap in your life. It's about reflecting on where you've been and setting your sights on where you want to go, then taking stock of the gap in between. It's really about looking at the story God is writing through your life to see what's transpired in light of His good purposes and to appreciate the ways He's redeemed the most painful situations. Seeing life through this lens really begins with believing that God is sovereign—meaning that He is all powerful (2 Samuel 7:22; Psalm 73:28). I don't know about you, but at times I've struggled with accepting this truth. I've doubted His love and faithfulness, especially amid devastating challenges—like my parents' divorce shortly after I graduated from college, or coming alongside one of my best friends as her husband battled brain cancer. However, the more years I walk with the Lord, the more I believe my mother-in-law's emphatic reminders that "God is sovereign!" And she should know, after having experienced twists, turns, and trials of all kinds.

It only takes looking at the story of Joseph in Genesis to be reminded of God's redemptive plans for what seem to be lowlights of our stories (Genesis 37:16–21). Although Joseph's brothers plotted to kill him, he didn't die in the cistern. God pulled him out of the pit and eventually used him to rescue the Israelites and save his own family: "You intended to harm me, but God intended it for good to accomplish what is now being done, the saving of many lives" (Genesis 50:20).

Joseph could have chosen to focus on the pit part of his story, recounting the hardship, pain, and suffering. Instead, he chose to remember his past in the context of God's purposes. That's what we need to do.

So let me ask you, what part of your story looks like the pit, and what would happen if you looked at it from God's vantage point?

Your past, present, and future circumstances all play a relevant part in the story God is writing through your life—a story meant to declare His work for others to see. Your story is never just about you. What has transpired in the gap of *what was* and *what is yet to be* is entirely significant to God and the purposes He has for using your absolutely unique and totally precious life.

> Your very lives are a letter that anyone can read by just looking at you.
> Christ himself wrote it—not with ink, but with God's living Spirit;
> not chiseled into stone, but carved into human lives—and we publish
> it. (2 Corinthians 3:3, MSG)

God can use for His glorious purposes even those parts of your story marred by pain—just as He did Joseph's. As I learned from Pastor James MacDonald during a week-long series at Camp-of-the-Woods in 2009, we all will find ourselves either in a trial, coming out of a trial, or about to head back into one (Matthew 6:34; Romans 8:17–18)![4] Our suffering—our painful trial—may be the result of a major trauma, like abuse, the betrayal of a spouse, or the death of a loved one, or it could be from something seemingly small, like unkind words at a critical time. It may be something done to us or something we do to ourselves. But regardless of the reason, only one response will lead us back to the Cross of Christ, where we can find His perspective as we ask God a life-changing question:

What do You want to accomplish for Your glory through this trial?

In other words, even in our suffering, we get to co-labor with God as He seeks to accomplish His purposes in us and often in others. While we might not understand what those purposes are at the time, when we come out of that season we will gain perspective and be positioned to tell that story for His glory.

Our stories can always be about Him.

So, my friend, how would you like to look at your life story while searching for God's redemptive glory?

From Salvation to Sanctification

Would you mind if I share part of my story with you before we dig further into yours? I hope it will help you see not only where I'm coming from but also give you a desire to pursue God in the writing of your story too.

As I mentioned, I've not always been interested in the business of living for God's glory. For the first twenty years of my life, I lived for me. I had one mission: grow up as fast as possible so that I could live life on my terms. While that might sound like a pretty normal endeavor for the average American teen, my desire was steeped in pain from the brokenness of my family, my own drive for self-preservation, and a strong will a mile wide.

My childhood was deeply affected by a legacy of abuse that dates back at least two generations. (By the grace of God, it ended when He healed me, and my family story has been totally redeemed.) My high-school and early college years were a mess, reflecting my choices to engage in reckless relationships, promiscuity, and foolish endeavors (too many to count). I was like an empty cup, longing to be filled up with love. But rather than going to the Source who could fill me completely— God Himself—I went from person to person, taking whatever I could get. It was never enough, because God didn't design any human being to be enough to complete another.

During the summer before my junior year of college, I began to understand that reality because of what I saw in the lives of some of my friends. I sensed that Jesus might be the answer, but I didn't know what to do about it, so I pushed the idea of faith aside. A month into my semester in London, I received a phone call from a close friend from home, Mr. Blue Eyes as I like to call him. It was one of those calls you never want to get—he shared with me that our friend's mom had lost her battle with cancer. I was in shock, as she was the first woman I had ever met whose faith was evident with every breath. She talked about Jesus and proclaimed His power in such a humble, winsome, convincing way. I was certain I would see her again on my return to the States—certain God would heal her because of her faith. Hearing the news of her death sent me into a crisis because I was forced to consider a fuller picture of the God I thought I might want to know better as well as what would happen to me when I died.

God felt a little closer and a whole lot farther away.

I wanted to secure my future, yet I didn't know if I could fully trust God with my life. I didn't get Him or understand how Mr. Blue Eyes could find peace in knowing our friend's mom was in heaven. He tried to answer my questions by sending me a Bible with key scriptures underlined, but I didn't understand what they meant. I headed upstairs to my friend Susie, whom I knew understood the Bible because she talked about it so much. I threw the Bible on the bed and asked for an explanation. I wanted to know how a loving, faithful woman would not have her prayer answered. Instead of answering me straight up, Susie posed a challenging question in the most loving of ways: "How do you think you get into heaven?"

I thought I had to be "good enough" in order to get my ticket to pass through the pearly gates, and I was pretty sure my entrance was not guaranteed. Susie didn't give my excuses much attention as she cut to the chase: "You don't need to be good enough to get into heaven. You simply need to believe that Jesus died on the cross for the forgiveness of your sins—all those things you've done that you know are wrong, and all that you'll ever do wrong in the future."

Really? This sounded too simple and yet totally appealing. All I had to do was believe that Jesus died for me to make me right with God and secure my spot in heaven (Romans 10:9–10; 1 John 1:9)? Susie pressed on, challenging me to think of the consequences. If she was right and I chose to accept Christ, we'd go to heaven together. If she was right and I refused to believe, I wasn't going to heaven when I died. And if she was wrong, well—we'd find out eventually. But did I want to risk the possibility of eternal life?

The promise of heaven was hope enough for me.

So that November evening, I decided that I was going to choose to believe that

Jesus died on the cross for the forgiveness of my sins and that by faith I would go to heaven when I died. It was all about the end goal for me, but much to my surprise, I discovered over time that God cares as much about our here and now as He does about eternity.

Life transformation may begin with salvation, but it doesn't end there.

There's so much more to my story, and I'm eager to share it with you in the days ahead, but for now know this: I've been walking with the Lord as my Savior for more than twenty years, and even so, I'm still in process. When you spend the first half of your life in an unhealthy pursuit of significance, it can take the second half of your life to undo all the wrong habits and false thinking you embraced as truth!

Regardless of where you are on your faith journey, God is in the middle of writing your story.

He is using the past while preparing for your future. The final destination is heaven, and every stop from here to there provides an opportunity to give God glory for His redemptive work in your life story. So how about taking time to mind the gap and harness new hope as you continue to pursue real life change?

Trap and Transform

Create Your Story Time Line

You're on this journey because you want to meet the new you. You want to move forward and find a new way of living. I understand. And I believe that is possible through God's transforming power. But before you can take the next step, you have to mind the gap between where you've been and where you want to go by taking stock of your life and looking through the lens of God's work. One way to do that concretely is by creating a time line of your life that includes the highlights, lowlights, and everything in between.

Step 1: Prepare the Time Line

Tape together three sheets of paper, end to end. Then draw a time line of your life from birth until present day—and be sure to include enough space to continue in the future.

Step 2: Record Key Dates and Events

Indicate the following as they pertain to you or other significant individuals in your life:

- Accomplishments
- Birth Dates
- Deaths
- Divorces
- Emotional Growth
- Graduations

- Moves
- Personal Development
- Times of Transition
- Trips
- Weddings

Step 3: Put on Spiritual Glasses

Record when your faith became your own, if you've had that experience, and the times and events in which you grew spiritually. You may also include any

Do You Want to Say Yes to God?

Friend, would you like to put your faith in Jesus Christ as your Savior, believing that He came to this earth as a babe, lived as fully man and fully God, and died on the cross to satisfy the debt of your sins before rising again? (Sin is any disobedience against God's instructions as they are found in the Bible.)

> If you declare with your mouth, "Jesus is Lord," and believe in your heart that God raised him from the dead, you will be saved. For it is with your heart that you believe and are justified, and it is with your mouth that you profess your faith and are saved. (Romans 10:9–10)

The Scriptures promise that when you put your faith in Jesus Christ, you are saved. That simply means that the door of heaven is opened to you personally.

> I am the door. If anyone enters by Me, he will be saved, and will go in and out and find pasture. The thief does not come except to steal, and

moments in which you can pinpoint God's rerouting of your plans and His redemptive power at work.

If this faith thing is new to you, maybe you would like to put a marker on your time line today. You can record something like *Seeking God* or draw a more permanent mark denoting your decision to live for God from this point forward.

Step 4: Mind the Gap Going Forward

Whether you've been walking with the Lord for as long as you can remember or have just turned in this new direction today, I encourage you to share your time line with others. You'll be inspired to continue to seek God for your future as you reflect on the dark places He's carried you through and the ways He has revealed Himself to you. Then your story will be an encouragement to others too as they see God at work in your life.

to kill, and to destroy. I have come that they may have life, and that they may have it more abundantly. (John 10:9–10, NKJV)

Putting your faith in Jesus also means that you receive the abundant life God promises. This doesn't mean a perfect life or one without suffering, but it does mean you've got God on your side. My friend, if this is what you want, then I encourage you to turn to God and say yes to His invitation by praying this confession:

Heavenly Father, I receive Your Son, Jesus Christ, as my Lord and
Savior, believing that He died on the cross for the forgiveness of my
sins. I ask You, Lord, to reveal to me more fully each day how Your
love is represented in the Cross and show me how to live fully for You
until I meet You face to face in heaven. In Jesus's name, amen.

Welcome to the family of God, friend, and to a most beautiful turning point in the story He is writing in your life.

Go Deeper

1. How does minding the gap—considering your present in light of your past while also looking toward the future—change your perspective on what God is accomplishing in your life?

2. Looking back on your life story, can you see times in which you had a plan for your future but God had something altogether different in mind? How did you respond? What was the outcome?

3. How might God want to use something from your past in a redemptive way in the future?

Give It Over

God, thank You for Your work in my life, even in the places where I cannot see Your purposes or Your presence. And thank You for where You are taking me in the future and the ways You want to transform me. I give You my life and ask You to order it. Please write Your story in my heart so that others might see Your glory. In Jesus's name, amen. (2 Corinthians 3:3)

Say Good-Bye to the "As Is" Life

Deal with Your Root Issues

I get to the heart of the human. I get
to the root of things.

—Jeremiah 17:10, msg

ave you begun to see areas of your life that need attention? Are you starting to recognize how pieces from the past might be influencing you today
and providing clues as to the story God is writing in your life? Well, my friend,
that's what's supposed to happen in this assessment phase. It's inventory time so that
you can pinpoint what you're working with. But remember this: nothing in your
life should be declared "as is," especially when God has the power to put His hands
on it.

Don't Be Duped by the "As Is" Clause

When my mother-in-law purchased her condo, we thought we did a good job reading the contract and figuring out the legalese. We even noticed the unusual com-
ment about the bedroom being "as is" and assumed that meant the built-in cabinet
would stay put, wonky drawers and all. So you can imagine our surprise when we
walked into her new home—no longer furnished with the former owners' belong-
ings—to discover that they had replaced the carpet only *around* where their queen

size waterbed had been, not under it. Aha! So that's what the contract meant by "as is."

"As is" means we have to deal with things the way they are—whether it's a condo or a used car, a clearance-priced piece of furniture or a chipped set of dishes.

While the objects in our lives might be "as is," we are not. As living, breathing human beings, we have the power to change.

While we're not "as is," we all have "as is" issues—the ones that pepper our lives with messes we'd rather sweep under the carpet. We often make excuses about them, like . . .

- *This is just the way God made me.*
- *I'm just stressed out and tired.*
- *If only I could change _____, I would be happy.*

Can you think of the excuse you use most often? Now let me ask you a tougher question: Does that excuse address the root issue? What do I mean by that? Up to this point, we've looked at your issues in terms of your circumstances and experiences in the context of what's happened *to* you, but now it's time to consider the part you've played. For example, perhaps your short temper is the core issue sabotaging your relationships. Maybe your battle with shame and guilt is holding you back from new opportunities. Or perhaps your bitterness is eroding your happiness. Since these types of root issues are keeping you from experiencing the change you crave, why not pinpoint them and deal with them head on?

Our root issues reflect the wounds and guilt buried deep inside. We like to pretend they don't exist, but they are often the sources of our problems. Unless we deal with them, they cause bigger problems. Every root issue is just like a dandelion! Did you know that if you try to pull a dandelion out of the ground, it will break off at the stem and leave the root behind—and that plant will just grow again? That's why you need a special tool that looks like a screwdriver with a pointed fork at the end. You have to get that tool right next to the stem and drive it down in the ground before pivoting it to pull up the dandelion by the root. Only then will that dandelion be gone for good. The same is true of your root issues.

So what's the right tool for getting to the heart of your issues? Well, it's not a *what* but a *who*—God. He is able to deal with the root, because He examines your heart and mind and knows everything.

But I, GOD, search the heart and examine the mind. I get to the heart of the human. I get to the root of things. I treat them as they really are, not as they pretend to be. (Jeremiah 17:10, MSG)

What a relief, right? God already knows all that you have stored up inside, and He is more than able to help you uncover those root issues so that you can heal from them. That's what He did for me, and I am fully convinced He wants to do it for you. Of course, we don't have the same story nor the same issues, but we do have the same, all-powerful, utterly amazing God who loves us dearly and wants to see His daughters transformed from the inside out.

WHEN GOD GOT TO MY ROOTS

Yesterday I shared with you the first part of my life-changing story, describing how God got my attention in London and saved my soul for eternity. It was an experience that rerouted my priorities and radically transformed my identity. But it took another ten years before I realized that I had given God only a part of me. It was as though I had taken everything ugly from my past and tried to bury it, but in reality, it was stored up in my heart and was wreaking havoc on my life. I was living like an "as is" woman instead of embracing the transformation process through the power and grace of God.

The appearance of "old" was certainly gone. I was no longer that partying, foul-mouthed college girl. Instead I was a churchgoing, Bible-reading, happily married momma of littles. I looked "new," but I felt battered and bruised, especially as I battled an unwelcome temper and a massive amount of insecurity. No matter how much I tried to change, nothing seemed to work. No amount of prayer, church attendance, or inspiring Bible study seemed to make a dent in my issues. What would it take to be transformed once and for all? Well, it turned out I needed a spiritual heart transplant brought on by a loving challenge set before me.

By God's grace, my husband called me out on my "as is" excuses: he pointed out how my anger and the words spewing out of my mouth reflected a disconnect between who I said I wanted to be as a follower of Christ and the way I was actually living. One of my best friends, Emily, had the courage to agree with him. Heeding

Emily's tender-loving advice, I recognized that I needed help dissecting my root issues and sought help from a godly counselor. As I began to unpack the events of my life—all thirty years of memories—I discovered my heart was hardened by wounds from long ago. My memories of the past were fueling my present-day responses. Rather than trying to forget about everything, I needed to face my issues head on and go in search of the root problems. With my counselor's leading and encouragement, I prayerfully sought God as I laid before Him this solitary question over and over again:

God, what do You have to say about this—this memory, this belief, this emotional response?

Sounds so simple, right? Actually, it was emotionally exhausting! I wept as I put words to every bit of pain, shame, and guilt I had stored up in my heart—things too painful and private to write about here. I didn't consider just what was done to me. I had to acknowledge what I had done too. I had carried around guilt over my promiscuity, the times I betrayed friends, all those years of lying to my parents about where I was and what I was doing, and more. While I was forgiven by God long ago, I didn't know how to release the pain and regret.

Finally, my heart broke open in the best of ways. Everything stored up inside poured out, and in return God showed me exactly where He had been: in the middle of my story. He surrounded me with His presence, and His mercy was a balm to my pain as He showed me that the wounds I had endured were not mine alone. They were His too.

When I suffered, God did too, for Christ's suffering was for me. The same is true for you.

The wounds I felt were the effects of sin—the very sin that pierced Jesus Christ as He hung on the cross. Finally, I came to see the loving, sacrificial gift of my Lord in a new light. I sensed how Jesus's arms had been wrapped around me long before I ever reached out mine to Him. What I had experienced in my past—all the pain and regret—was only a portion of what it could have been, because Christ was taking it first and fully.

Seeing my suffering in light of the Cross changed my perspective. Suddenly I felt His peace as He enabled me to release the guilt and shame. As Dee Brestin writes in the *The God of All Comfort,* this matter of suffering is a mystery:

This is what the Lord asks. To accept the mystery of suffering. To trust the heart of the One who died for us. He has a reason for suffering, and one day it will be made clear.[5]

Yes, I suffered. And I am sure you have too. Regardless of the magnitude of what we've been through, the truth is that God sees all of it and He can heal it. Our suffering is not the end of our stories. The cross on which Christ died was not the end of His either. The good news of the gospel is that He rose again. He overcame the grave. In Christ, we have healing power at work in our lives, redeeming the pain in our stories too.

Friend, it's all too easy to strive after living for the Lord while keeping our hearts from Him—and yet our wounded hearts, resistant to God's love, are the sources of so many difficulties in our lives.

Giving God your past doesn't erase it but rather enables God to redeem it.

As God opened my eyes to see His presence in my past, He also entered my heart in a new way. It's as if I gave Him permission to dwell in all of me instead of only in the parts I thought were acceptable. Do you know what happened? The bitterness I struggled with dissipated. The critical spirit waned. The insecurity lessened. And that awful temper, which I thought I'd never get rid of, began to fade away.

Yes, it took time and much discipline on my part, as I saw God daily, asking Him again and again to speak truth over my beliefs and emotions. I had to learn how to think differently in order to act differently, and that started with letting God into the inmost parts of my beliefs.

Gone is the yelling lunatic and crazed mom my children once knew. Praise the Lord! Instead they have a momma who might still lose her cool but not like a banshee wigging out over spilled milk. (Or, at least not without owning the banshee moment when that old woman tries to resurrect herself.)

Those "as is" issues are dissipating, my friend, in an ongoing process of transformation. There will always be some hurt ready to spring a root and entangle our hearts in an ugly mess. That's why we have to continually yield our hearts to Him and choose to embrace His truth, which is exactly the point Karen Ehman makes in *Let It Go:*

What transforms our outlook and us is an attitude shift. It's God's job to determine our circumstances. It's our job to cooperate with him in the midst of them, adjusting and realigning our attitudes with the truth of Scripture.[6]

Yes, transformation begins with an attitude shift, and that happens when we give God inner access to our most secret thoughts by being honest with Him. So will you embrace this next step of taking a hard look at your "as is" issues to identify the roots that are bearing the fruit you'd like to cut out of your life for good?

Trap and Transform

From Root to Fruit

Don't worry, I don't expect you to tackle all your issues at once! Rather, as we've been doing all week, let's take inventory to discover the right next steps.

Step 1: What's Your Fruit?

Which of these undesirable fruits are manifest in your life? For each one you check off, describe the circumstances in which you feel or behave that way.

- ❏ Anger
- ❏ Bickering
- ❏ Bitterness
- ❏ Criticism
- ❏ Gossip
- ❏ Jealousy
- ❏ Malice
- ❏ Manipulation
- ❏ Rage
- ❏ Revenge
- ❏ Slander
- ❏ Unforgiveness

Step 2: What Are the Roots?

Looking at the list, can you see root issues? For example, the fruit of bitterness may be the by-product of a betrayal from years ago. See if you can pinpoint the fruits with the roots in your life.

Step 3: What Do You Need to Do About It?

Whether you've experienced major hurts (abuse, death of a loved one, any life-altering change) or little ones (a rupture in a friendship, a time when you were overlooked for a promotion, any minor disappointment that knocked the wind out of you for a time), you may need the wisdom and care of a professional counselor to help you process the impact. If pain lingers in your heart for months and months, that's when you know there is a root issue that needs tending.

- If you identified some *minor* root issues, what is the next step you will take to deal with those issues?

- Did you discover some *major* root issues? What step do you want to take to pursue healing?

Go Deeper

1. What would life look like if your root issues no longer had a stronghold on you? For example, if your battle with anger was resolved by dealing

with the root issue of unforgiveness, how would that impact your life? Jot down your thoughts about your root issues as they are now and how life would be different if they were no longer marking your life.

2. What is your number one root issue that needs dealing with? What's the first step you'll take to deal with that issue?

3. What are your apprehensions about getting help to deal with issues you haven't been able to solve on your own? What's the cost of not getting help?

Give It Over

Heavenly Father, I know my tendency is to pretend my issues are not a big deal—or even issues at all. Please forgive me for hiding and running from You. Lord, enable me to walk upright before You, embracing the process of dealing with my root issues so that the fruit in my life will give glory to You. In Jesus's name, amen. (Jeremiah 17:9–10)

Phase 2

Assess the Goods

Deep spiritual growth requires
giving attention to the whole
person—emotional, relational,
physical, and spiritual.

—Robert S. McGee

You're Made New

Understand Who You Are

The old has gone, the new is here!

—2 CORINTHIANS 5:17

I f I asked you to introduce yourself to someone, what would you say? Would you refer to the roles you fill: "Hi, I'm a wife and mom" or "I work for so-and-so"? Would you mention the things you're passionate about or what you've recently accomplished, like completing a half marathon (and then I might glare at you jealously)? Would you mention your dream to start a business, even though you've not done a lick of work on it in the last month? Or would you refer to your temperament, describing a tendency to be a take-charge type of gal or one that prefers to serve behind the scenes?

It's interesting that we define ourselves by what we do and how we live, whereas God defines us by who we are in light of what He's done.

Imagine if you shifted your focus from an identity defined by your behavior and began thinking about your life in light of your God-given worth as His child. How would that perspective influence the way you approach your life? And as a result, what attitudes and habits would naturally be transformed?

TAKE OFF THAT HORRID COAT

Viking. That was my identity for the first thirty-something years of my life. Where did that label come from? Well, my mom teasingly said I was born angry like a

Viking, and I believed it. Why wouldn't I, considering my hot-tempered, sharp-tongued, combative personality?

Looking back, I can see how my Viking-like reactions were fueled by the dysfunction in my family and were a by-product of my God-given personality (something we'll explore more tomorrow). The fact is, I wasn't born angry. I was born strong willed with a huge bent for righting wrongs—thus my rebellious reaction to the dysfunctions I experienced. Going through the healing process with the Lord softened my temperament yet didn't immediately change my perception of myself. For years, I felt like a Viking in disguise.

I wanted to be a changed woman on the inside and outside.

I wanted to be authentic, not masked.

I wanted to be kind, gentle, patient, and self-controlled.

The struggle to find the real me—the woman I believed God wanted me to become—drove me to prayer, time and time again. I begged the Lord to change me. To make me new. I told Him I didn't want to be like this any longer, yet I often felt like I would never be fully changed. And then one desperate morning after an explosive encounter with my family the previous night, God set me free with the truth and revealed how to move forward:

> *I already made you new when you put your life in My hands and trusted in My Son as your Savior. When you confessed your sins to Me, I gave you a fresh start. I made you new, but you're not living like it. You're living like the old you.*
>
> *It's as if you're wearing this matted, skanky fur coat. It's like a garment you refuse to take off, even though it is heavy and smelly. You think it is who you are. But it's not. It's time to take it off, even if you feel exposed. It's time to shed the old you and live as the new you I created you to become.*

I could smell *that* smell and see *that* coat in vivid, three-dimensional color. And I wanted to get rid of it like nobody's business.

> *Yes, Lord. Yes! I trust You to cover me as I take off this stench from my past and walk forward as the new woman You designed me to be.*

In that moment, something happened inside my soul. I believed God about this truth and I wanted to live it out. But could I? Would I forget by the afternoon? That was my fear! I felt I needed some sort of reminder, so I did something that made my life more complicated but more precious. I dropped the *E* from my name, not formally or legally, but in conversation with family, friends, and colleagues . . . and in introductions.

"Instead of calling me Elisa, call me Lisa."

In the same way God changed Abram to Abraham, Sarai to Sarah, and Saul to Paul, I felt that the Lord's grace was upon me and it was okay, even a good idea, for me to go by a new name too—as a reminder to live that new life God had set apart for me.

I finally believed in my heart and mind that I was fully free to live as a new creation, not forgetting my past, but moving on from it as I embraced my true identity as God's totally redeemed child:

> Therefore, if anyone is in Christ, the new creation has come: The old has
> gone, the new is here! (2 Corinthians 5:17)

Remarkably, miraculously, I experienced a deep transformation in my soul as I chose to believe the truth about who I am in His sight . . .

Chosen. Holy. Dearly loved. Called. Qualified. Accepted. One of a kind.

These new labels—these scripturally sound truths—were calling me to live out my Christ-centered identity instead of defining myself by my behavior, roles, feelings, and failures. These identity truths beckoned me to a new way of living.

Is it time for you to embrace a new identity too?

You Are Chosen

In God's eyes, you are far more than what you see in the mirror or strive to accomplish in a given day. You are not defined by what you do or don't do, but by whose you are—His holy and dearly loved daughter, set apart for a divinely appointed purpose.

> You are the ones chosen by God, chosen for the high calling of priestly
> work, chosen to be a holy people, God's instruments to do his work and

speak out for him, to tell others of the night-and-day difference he made for you—from nothing to something, from rejected to accepted. (1 Peter 2:9–10, MSG)

You are a chosen, beloved child of God, set apart for His glorious purposes.

Friend, no matter how you see yourself, God sees you through His perfect Son, Jesus Christ. Imagine if you started looking at your life from that vantage point! Your identity is found in knowing who you are as His child and believing that belonging to Him matters most of all. You are His instrument, meant to sing out His praises.

Yes, you're imperfect. But Christ is perfect. Yes, you're a sinner. But in Christ, your sins have been forgiven. Yes, you're unkind. But in Christ, you come before a compassionate and merciful God who can overflow kindness from within your soul. Yes, you're wounded. But Christ has come to redeem and heal those wounds as He makes you holy and whole.

Christ's covering shapes your truest identity.

You are not defined by the roles you fill or the responsibilities with which you're charged. It doesn't matter if you're married, single, divorced, or widowed. If you're a work-at-an-office mom, a work-from-home mom, a stay-at-home mom, or a home-schooling mom. It doesn't make a difference in God's eyes if you're college educated or successful in your career. These roles are not a reflection of who you are, nor are the labels you feel most familiar wearing, such as *pretty* or *smart* or *cranky* or *critical* or *angry* or *insecure.* You can fulfill all sorts of roles, accomplish all sorts of things, and assume all sorts of labels, but none of them define your identity in Christ.

Trap and Transform

Discover Your True Identity

Your God-given identity is incredibly multifaceted, describing who you are regardless of how you feel about yourself. It is true, no matter what you believe about yourself or God or the relevance of the Word. So I encourage you to soak up these scriptural truths, reading them slowly, one by one. Consider how believing these truths could change your life. As you continue this journey, take time to read each Scripture reference in the context of the chapter. Jot down what each truth means to you personally.

1. I am chosen by God. (Ephesians 1:4–11)

2. I am God's child. (Romans 8:14–15)

3. I am Christ's friend. (John 15:14–15)

4. I am God's workmanship. (Ephesians 2:10, NKJV)

5. I am God's coworker. (2 Corinthians 6:1)

6. I am chosen and appointed to bear His fruit. (John 15:16)

7. I am forgiven. (Matthew 26:28; Ephesians 1:7)

8. I am sealed with the promised Holy Spirit. (Ephesians 1:13)

9. I am a new creation. (2 Corinthians 5:17)

10. I am alive with Christ. (Ephesians 2:5)

11. I am blessed. (Ephesians 1:3)

12. I am set free. (Romans 8:2)

13. I am not afraid. (Isaiah 43:1–3)

14. I am never alone. (Deuteronomy 31:6–8)

15. I am able to walk by faith, not by sight. (2 Corinthians 5:7)

16. I am victorious through the Lord Jesus Christ. (1 Corinthians 15:57)

17. I am not controlled by the sinful nature but by the Spirit. (Romans 8:9)

18. I cannot be snatched out of God's hand. (John 10:28)

19. I am able to hear God's voice. (John 8:47)

20. I do not belong to this world. (John 15:19)

21. I belong to God! (1 Peter 2:9)

Go Deeper

1. What experiences and relationships have influenced your identity? How did they form labels that you're no longer meant to wear?

2. Which identity truths from Scripture mean the most to you today? Which ones are the hardest to accept?

3. How does considering your God-given identity change your perspective about how you want to live?

Give It Over

Heavenly Father, help me to move forward in my identity as Your child. Help me to see the new woman You've made me to become as I let go of the past and move into the future. Show me how to embrace the fact that You have chosen me, loved me, and set me apart to accomplish Your purposes in this world. In Jesus's name, amen. (2 Corinthians 5:17; 1 Peter 2:9)

A Complete Package

Embrace Your Strengths and Weaknesses

My grace is sufficient for you, for my
power is made perfect in weakness.

—2 Corinthians 12:9

Have you ever considered the intricacies of how God made you? I'm not referring to the color of your hair (yes, the original shade) or the shape of your body. I'm not even thinking about the intonation of your accent, y'all, or your fashionista style. I'm talking about why you think and act the way you do—whether you march into a room and start barking orders or slip behind the crowd and hope no one notices you. Maybe you can plop down at a desk and start working with piles stacked high, or maybe you'd have to spend the first twenty minutes clearing a space in order to function well. Maybe you're the first one to respond to a crisis or the last one to show up at a social event, finding every excuse as to why staying home and reading a book is a better idea.

Friend, these tendencies reflect your God-given personality, which includes both your strengths and weaknesses, so let's find out how God intends to use the *complete you* to accomplish His purposes.

UNDERSTANDING THE PERSONALITY TYPES

Have you ever considered the amazing ways God has wired our personalities? Each one of us has a different way we go about doing life and connecting with others—

whether we like to be social or alone, leading or following, creating or analyzing, planning or preparing. These personality traits manifest themselves in the ways we maintain our homes, pursue jobs, respond to conflict, and engage in relationships. They not only influence our choices, but they also impact those we're closest to. That's why studying the personality types is incredibly valuable: it not only helps you connect the dots of why you do what you do, but it also helps you understand others better.

My favorite personality assessment is one created by Marita and Florence Littauer, authors of *Wired That Way,* because they use four simple categories we relate to easily, with an overall focus on how the different personality types, which include distinctive strengths and weaknesses, are reflected in the body of Christ:

- Sanguine: the social butterfly and life of the party
- Choleric: the focused leader who can also be easily angered
- Melancholy: the sensitive, creative type who likes everything in order
- Phlegmatic: the laid-back observer who prefers to hang out behind the scenes[7]

Other popular assessments, which go beyond personalities, include these:

- The JUNG, based on the research of Carl Jung, classifies people as introverts or extroverts, then also considers judging and perceiving functions of each individual. This system uses letter combinations such as ESTJ, which stand for Extraversion (E), Sensing (S), Thinking (T), and Judgment (J).[8]
- The Myers-Briggs Type Indicator (MBTI) is built from Jung's research and divides the temperaments according to four preference pairs—Extraversion (E) or Introversion (I), Sensing (S) or Intuition (N), Thinking (T) or Feeling (F) , and Judging (J) or Perceiving (P).[9]
- The DISC, established by psychologist William Moulton Marston, looks at behavior from the perspective of Dominance, Inducement, Submission, and Compliance.[10]
- The StrengthsFinder measures talents and abilities in the context of strengths in leadership.[11]
- The Highlands Company provides a comprehensive battery that considers abilities, skills, interests, personal style, family background, values, goals, and career development to help cultivate personal vision.[12]

These eye-opening assessments reveal how God has made us unique and that there is no perfect personality; rather, everyone has a combination of strengths and weaknesses. By doing several assessments, you also discover that while God has wired your personality, it has also been shaped by your environment and sometimes even masked—meaning that because of the influence of a strong or controlling personality or the effects of a particular traumatic experience, who God made you to be and how you actually respond and relate to others is in conflict. When I finally discovered that my personality had been masked, the internal conflict between my natural preferences and "the right way" of doing things finally had an explanation and beautiful resolution.

Let me give you a few examples related to my mom and me. We have nearly opposite personality types. I have a strong sanguine bent, which means I love every thing bright, bold, and fashionably new. However, my mom is a strong melancholy, which means she would choose a shirt that is practical, comfortable, and timeless over one that is trendy and blingy with sequins. Because I respect my mom so much and see great value in how she lives life, I want to emulate her, and yet her way is not my way. So when I go shopping, my sanguine self might grab a "loud" shirt on my way to the checkout—but by the time I get home, the melancholy voice I know so well urges me to make a more practical choice. That's why I used to head back to the store and make a beeline for the returns desk—until I finally realized that there are times when my sanguine side could and should play the trump card.

It's not only in shopping that we're different.

You should see my mom's lovely home. It's so clean and simple, with every speck of dirt banished and every nook in order. I've learned so much from her, and I do try to imitate her good housekeeping habits. Yet although my home is just as comfortable, it's not like hers. It's tidy-ish. Clean-ish. But don't look behind the closet doors, especially during a busy week, since I'm Queen Shover, raising a family of shovers, much to my dismay.

For years I thought, *If only I were more like my mom, I'd spend less time in return lines and more time tackling the dust bunnies threatening to overtake my home.* It wasn't until I recognized how our personality types shaped our different approaches to life that I was finally freed to do life my way, without feeling guilty or "less than."

Wouldn't it be nice for you to get comfortable living the way God made you, while learning from others and inviting Him to work in your weaknesses too?

What to Do with Weaknesses

Did you know that if you got rid of all your weaknesses—those aspects of your personality that you don't like—you'd have to wipe out the related strength too, because a weakness may simply mask an unbridled strength?

Through parenting my middle daughter, Abby, I've come to see how we are complete packages. Abby's God-given wiring is vibrant and prone to sparks, if you know what I mean. She's a leader type (code for *strong-willed*), along with being a servant-hearted girl who is always prepared. Her ability to plan ahead became clear to me when she was only nine. It was just beginning to rain as we were heading to a department store, and she said, "Don't worry, Mom, I brought an umbrella!" I chuckled under my breath as she reached into her bag of tricks. Just then, her little sister said, "I'm thirsty!" and her brother said, "I'm hungry." Like Mary Poppins, Abby whipped a water bottle and granola bar out of her bottomless bag. *Oh my, who taught her to be so prepared, so resourceful?*

Not me! All I had was a wallet on a string and a cell phone. I gave up carrying gear long ago! I suppose when Abby was little, she might have learned the value of being prepared from watching me, but honestly, she owns this thing in such a way that I know it's how God made her. I'm equally convinced it's how He'll use her too, as long as she's willing to submit to His way over her way. See, Abby's strength of being prepared has a counterpart weakness of being irritable when things don't go according to her plan. She can become quite *sparky* when her sense of being in control and following through with meeting needs goes awry. When that happens, it's natural to think that she (ahem, we) should focus on eradicating the weakness (a need to be in control), but the truth is that her weakness is a counterpart to her strength (being insightful enough and prepared to meet needs). And this is a good thing.

God made us with a need for Him, and by His grace, He promises to show up and work His wonder in us through our weaknesses.

I know it's upside-down thinking to see a weakness from this perspective, but as Bible-study teacher Priscilla Shirer says, this is God's method:

> Weakness is a key, and like most keys, it's designed to open something. God designed your key specifically to fit the lock He has in mind for you. He

uses your weaknesses, the areas and places where you feel the least strong, to open a divine door. Without this key, we would rarely experience God's strength.[13]

What we really need to learn how to do is yield our weaknesses and strengths to God. For example, what if Abby developed a habit of praying, *God, I'm feeling irritable about this plan not working out. Please help me to trust You with the details.* Imagine how God might work through her yielded heart and open hands. Her temperament would settle as she puts her trust in the Lord, and in the process her faith would grow too. Can you imagine what God might want to accomplish through your strengths *and* weaknesses as you yield both to Him?

God will use you, but you need to be usable, even in your weaknesses.

God needs creative, solution-minded women and analytical deep thinkers. He needs social butterflies and people connectors along with reserved, one-on-one types. He needs planners and visionaries as well as detailed-oriented folks who want to get their hands dirty.

Like thorns in your side, your weaknesses may gnaw at you, but as Paul described, it may be God's intention for you to learn how to live with them so that you depend all the more on Him:

> In order to keep me from becoming conceited, I was given a thorn in my flesh, a messenger of Satan, to torment me. Three times I pleaded with the Lord to take it away from me. But he said to me, "My grace is sufficient for you, for my power is made perfect in weakness." Therefore I will boast all the more gladly about my weaknesses, so that Christ's power may rest on me. That is why, for Christ's sake, I delight in weaknesses, in insults, in hardships, in persecutions, in difficulties. For when I am weak, then I am strong. (2 Corinthians 12:7–10)

Because of that thorn, the apostle Paul came face to face with the power of God, seeing Him at work in his weakness. So shall you and I. Paul didn't run or deny or dismiss the reality of his thorn. He gave it to God and asked for help . . . a solution . . . a way out. God sees your thorns, and He has a plan for how to work through them.

Trap and Transform

Embrace Your Personality Type

Are you ready to figure out the creative way God has wired your personality and to pinpoint your strengths and weaknesses? I recommend you complete a couple of different assessments and read all the feedback so that you can get a full picture. Remember, you're not getting graded in the assessments, and you can't fail. It's simply an opportunity for discovery and growth.

Step 1: Take an Assessment

Free Assessments:

- 16Personalities: www.16personalities.com. View the visual interpretation of JUNG/MBTI results here: www.cpp.com /contents/type-heads.aspx.
- TypeFinder: www.truity.com/test/type-finder-research-edition. View different types at www.truity.com/view/types.
- DISC: www.123test.com/disc-personality-test. View types at www.123test.com/disc-profiles.

For-Fee Assessments:

- Wired That Way: http://classervices.com/shopsite_sc/store /html/page1.html
- StrengthsFinder: www.gallupstrengthscenter.com/Purchase /en-US/Index
- Highlands Ability Battery: www.highlandsco.com or www .elisapulliam.com/highlands

Step 2: Reflect on the Results

1. What did you discover about your personality?

2. Can you pinpoint who or what shaped your personality?

3. How does discovering your personality type change the way you see yourself?

Step 3: What Are Your Strengths and Weaknesses?

Jot down your top five strengths and their correlating weaknesses.

	Strength	Weakness
1.	_____	_____
2.	_____	_____
3.	_____	_____
4.	_____	_____
5.	_____	_____

Ask the Lord to show you how to surrender your strengths to His purposes and yield your weaknesses to His power. Jot down your prayers and any revelation the Lord gives to you:

Go Deeper

1. What about your personality do you like? What would you change?

2. As you look at your strengths, can you see how you've been perfectly made for certain roles or opportunities? Explain.

3. Which of your weaknesses requires immediate attention? Whom can you seek out for guidance in this area?

Give It Over

Lord God, may I learn how to embrace the way You made me, even my weaknesses, so that I may experience Your power being made perfect in my life. May I always use my strengths for Your kingdom purposes. Show me, Lord, how to appreciate the strengths and weaknesses in others too, and allow me to learn from their examples. In Jesus's name, amen. (2 Corinthians 12:9)

Satisfyingly Good

Discover Your Talents and Spiritual Gifting

Each of you should use whatever gift
you have received to serve others.

—1 Peter 4:10

𝒜re you starting to see how beneficial it is to uncover your God-given identity and personality? Hopefully, your new understanding is beginning to
put your life into perspective and give you glimpses of what might be ahead. Today
we'll look at refining that vision by considering how your talents and gifting can be
used in a fully satisfying, God-ordained way.[14]

What's a Talent?

A talent is a natural ability, like being able to sing on key, twirl a baton (does anyone
do that anymore?), decorate a house on a shoestring budget, or make sweet-tooth-
happy desserts (like my friend Stacie's chocolate-chip cookies with an Oreo baked
inside . . . yum). Typically, a talent is something you have a knack for, and yet it can
also be something you cultivate and perfect over time with training. You can certainly use it to honor God and bless others while enjoying it yourself.

A talent shouldn't be defined by whether it earns applause.

We all have talents but don't always recognize them as such, especially when we compare our talents to those of the people around us. It takes talent to be able to teach a nine-year-old how to draw a horse. It's a talent to be able to redesign and rebuild a fireplace mantel—yes, I have a friend who did this all by herself. It's a talent to be able to organize a storage closet. It even takes talent to cultivate a ministry from the ground up or launch a business.

Even if others don't notice or appreciate your particular talent, God values it because He gave it to you.

Can you think of a talent God has given you that you have devalued, neglected, or simply ignored? Do you find yourself coming up with excuses to justify why you shouldn't enjoy a particular talent? Is fear of the scrutiny of others at the top of the list?

Too many women forsake enjoying their talents because they feel frivolous using them. That was my struggle until God freed me of it one ordinary afternoon when I should have been catching up on sleep. The twins were down for their nap and the girls were off at school, so I plopped down on the couch, hoping to rest. Instead, my creative juices were flowing as a vision of a red flower took shape in my mind, so I decided to seize the moment. I dug out my painting supplies for the first time since my college years and cleared the Ping-Pong table to set up a work-space. Of course I needed a canvas, so I grabbed a frame and decided the back of the mounting board would suffice. Three hours later (the twins always rocked their afternoon nap), the girls arrived home from school with their nana . . . just in time to find me putting the last stroke of color on the largest canvas I'd ever painted. That painting became a precious reminder to me to use the talent God has given me for the sheer pleasure of it.

What would it look like for you to enjoy your God-given talents without having to use them for a particular purpose? Consider how a little investment of time in nurturing your talents could breathe life into your soul.

IT'S A SPIRITUAL GIFT WHEN . . .

While a talent may be steeped in pleasure, a spiritual gift is even richer because God designed it to encourage and equip His children to accomplish His purposes. God specifically gives each one of us a gift with His greater plans in mind—we don't get to choose our gifting, although we can learn the skills woven into the gifts by watching those who are operating in their gifting. So what are the spiritual gifts? Scripture describes them in a number of passages, with the most elaborate explanation in 1 Corinthians 12:

> God's various gifts are handed out everywhere; but they all originate in God's Spirit. God's various ministries are carried out everywhere; but they all originate in God's Spirit. God's various expressions of power are in action everywhere; but God himself is behind it all. Each person is given something to do that shows who God is: Everyone gets in on it, everyone benefits. All kinds of things are handed out by the Spirit, and to all kinds of people! The variety is wonderful:
>
>   wise counsel
>   clear understanding
>   simple trust
>   healing the sick
>   miraculous acts
>   proclamation
>   distinguishing between spirits
>   tongues
>   interpretation of tongues.

All these gifts have a common origin, but are handed out one by one by the one Spirit of God. He decides who gets what, and when. . . .

I want you to think about how all this makes you more significant, not less. A body isn't just a single part blown up into something huge. It's all the different-but-similar parts arranged and functioning together. . . .

But I also want you to think about how this keeps your significance from getting blown up into self-importance. For no matter how significant you are, it is only because of what you are a *part* of. . . .

You are Christ's body—that's who you are! You must never forget this. Only as you accept your part of that body does your "part" mean anything.

You're familiar with some of the parts that God has formed in his church, which is his "body":

apostles
prophets
teachers
miracle workers
healers
helpers
organizers
those who pray in tongues. (verses 4–11, 14, 19, 27–28, MSG)

But what does this all mean? By drawing upon the four main passages of Scripture that reference the spiritual gifts—Romans 12:4–8; 1 Corinthians 12; 1 Corinthians 14; Ephesians 4:11–13—and looking at multiple translations (NIV, NLT, TLB, and MSG), you can glean a general sense of the types of gifts and how they are used:

- An *apostle* plants churches and spreads the gospel.
- An *evangelist* tells people the gospel.
- A *prophet* speaks the truth as led by the Holy Spirit.
- A *pastor/shepherd* cares for the faith of God's people.
- A *helper* generously, practically meets needs.
- A *teacher* studies and teaches the Word.
- An *encourager* feels compelled to spur people on in their faith.
- A *leader* diligently governs with vision and clarity of direction.
- An *administrator* performs tasks and organizes people to get the job done.
- A *merciful person* shows compassion to the hurting and those in need.
- A *healer* brings healing to those emotionally, physically, and spiritually wounded.
- A *person who speaks in tongues* uses a special prayer language and/or interprets it for others.
- A *faith-filled person* unwaveringly believes in God's abilities.
- A *discerner* distinguishes truth from lies.
- A *wise person* makes the Word relevant to life.

Maybe you've heard some of these descriptions before. Maybe you can even see where you fit. Or maybe you're like me when I first heard about the spiritual gifts as a newbie Christian. I was excited about how they would help me understand my life purpose, but I wasn't mature enough in my faith (or in life, for that matter) to see how any of these giftings described me. Even after doing the assessments, I was miffed by the results. How could I be a teacher or discerner of the truth when I didn't even know it? I even changed my major in college from elementary education to English and art because I didn't want to teach. Isn't that ironic?

Twenty years later, I can see that the spiritual-gifts assessment I took was spot on: I do have gifts of discernment, prophecy, and teaching, but I only began to see them manifested in my life as I became serious about studying the Word and saying yes to opportunities to speak, first to teen girls and later to women's groups. I'm sure this is God's gifting at work in me because when I get up to speak, the words flow from my lips even though I struggle with memorization and I'm terrified about being in front of people.

I encourage you to give yourself time to recognize the ways spiritual gifts manifest themselves in your life. And more importantly, to be willing to learn from others who share a similar gifting as well as from those who have a gift that is totally different from yours. For example, my husband and our middle daughter, Abby, are both gifted with mercy, hospitality, and serving. I've learned so much from watching them use their gifting that people actually think it's my gifting too. Oh no! But I can put those skills to work to serve in a way that is not my natural bent. As you study the spiritual gifts and watch them play out in others, it will become obvious why we need one another!

So how do you know which spiritual gifting God has given you and how to use it? You can figure it out in a couple of ways, including taking spiritual-gift assessments, asking others what they see in you, and evaluating how you function in settings where a spiritual gift might be used. But before pinpointing your gifting, let's look at the why behind it.

It's Meant to Be Given

The greatest mistake we can make when studying spiritual gifts is to expect that our God-given gifting is for our own gain. It's not. Our gifting allows us to serve others so that God's purposes prevail. It's about saying yes to those God has called us to serve, using whatever gift He has given us:

> Each of you should use whatever gift you have received to serve others,
> as faithful stewards of God's grace in its various forms. (1 Peter 4:10)

God doesn't ask us to be the best at using our gifts but to focus on demonstrating His love toward others through operating as He designed. We get to use our spiritual gifts as vehicles of His love.

The way you use the gifts is more important than the gifts themselves.

They are created to be used in the context of love. Paul made this clear in 1 Corinthians 13, the passage that follows the list of spiritual gifts. In essence, he said,

- An evangelist without love is a clanging symbol.
- A prophet without love is a critical spirit.
- A teacher without love is harsh and insulting.

A gift being used without love is not a gift at all. So, as you uncover your spiritual gifts, keep this question in mind: *How can I use these gifts to express God's love to others?*

Trap and Transform

Discover Your Spiritual Gifts

I recommend using both of these free online assessments in order to see a well-rounded picture of your spiritual gifts:

- SpiritualGiftsTest.com: www.spiritualgiftstest.com/test/adult
- ChurchGrowth.com: www.churchgrowth.org/cgi-cg/gifts .cgi?intro=1

Keep in mind that your results may be skewed, depending on how you've been influenced by your church upbringing, current community, family, and the culture. If you're bewildered by the results, spend time studying the descriptions of the gifts and ask the Lord to provide opportunities to experiment with using your perceived gifts. Also seek the input of friends and family, as they may be able to see your giftings at work better than you can.

One more thing to consider: as you look at the ways you currently serve, where you work, and how you function at home, consider the areas of frustration as well as times in which you feel true satisfaction. These are clues to your gifting. If you are skilled at a task but don't enjoy doing it, that might be a sign you're not operating in your gifting. In contrast, a task that falls within your gifting is something you enjoy and feel like you could do every day.

Step 1: What Is Your Gifting?
Based on your assessments, what are your primary and secondary gifts?

1. _____

2. _____

Step 2: Surrender and Yield
As you look at your spiritual gifts in light of your life commitments and relationships, consider these questions:

1. Can you determine how God is leading you to use your gifting in your church, family, community, work, or ministry?

2. What steps do you need to take to make more intentional use of your spiritual gifts?

3. Knowing your spiritual gifting, do you see why you might be frustrated with a particular role or responsibility? How could you transition out of that role or responsibility into one that lines up with your gifts?

Go Deeper

1. What talents do you feel God has given you? How can you make time to enjoy them without feeling guilty?

2. When you consider the spiritual gifting God has given you, can you see ways in which He is calling you to use it?

3. How does thinking about your talents and gifts change how you see your life purpose?

Give It Over

Heavenly Father, thank You for giving me both natural talents and spiritual gifting. Please, Lord, show me how to receive what You've given with open arms and a desire to use my gifts as an outpouring of Your love. Remind me, Lord, not to use my gifting for my own gain but for Your people and purposes. In Jesus's name, amen. (1 Corinthians 12–13; 1 Peter 4:10)

Set Apart with Distinction

The Impact of Learning Styles

I am fearfully and wonderfully made.

—Psalm 139:14

This week has been all about discovering your God-given wiring so that you can face the future with the knowledge of how you're made. Today, we're going one step further by considering how you learn. Why? Because when you lack confidence about your intelligence, it undermines God's purposes for your life. Also, your learning style impacts the way you approach new opportunities and carry out your responsibilities.

What, I'm Not Stupid?

I remember that day in sixth grade when I discovered I might not know everything. The sun shone brightly through the classroom window, and the blue sky stood stark against the fall foliage. My daydreaming was rudely interrupted by the teacher passing back our math tests. When I saw that giant, red-letter F, I choked back tears. It was the first failing mark I'd ever received. In fact, I had straight As the year before— even as a brand-new student to the school and placed in a classroom of troubled kids.

Something devastating happened in that moment as I allowed a grade to define my sense of worth.

From that point forward, I believed I was stupid. I quit trying, not only in math but in other areas too. One bad grade led to a confidence downfall, even though all I needed were some study tips and practice memorizing basic concepts. Unfortunately, my teachers and parents missed the cues—and I refused to ask for help. That F shaped how I thought of myself *for the next twenty years,* until a transformational moment occurred at a parent-teacher conference for my oldest daughter. While I thought the appointment was supposed to be about how Leah was doing in first grade, God had something else in mind. Mrs. Esposito and I reviewed her report card and standardized-test scores, which revealed that Leah didn't lack in the intelligence department.

"Obviously, she got all her brains from her dad's side of the family."

Yep, that's exactly what I said to Mrs. Esposito. I expected her to nod in agreement. Instead, she pushed aside those papers and looked straight into my eyes. "Honey, she's half you and half your husband. He's not the only bright one in the bunch."

Until Mrs. Esposito uttered those words of truth, I really did believe I was half—half of the problem. Have you struggled with feeling not good enough when it comes to your smarts? Did a grade or assessment of some kind reroute your dreams and your beliefs about your potential? Have you let a rejection from an honors program or a waitlist from a college define you? When you didn't get that job or were overlooked for that promotion, did you feel as if you should just quit? Did someone you respect carelessly imply that you were "less than" in a particular area of life?

Isn't it amazing how one moment can forever impact what you believe about yourself? Friend, I have good news for you: it doesn't have to stay that way. The beauty of God's redemptive work is that He can undo even decades of damaged thinking with one word of truth.

The truth is that God made you fearfully and wonderfully, not frightfully and worthlessly.

> I praise you because I am fearfully and wonderfully made;
>> your works are wonderful,
>> I know that full well. (Psalm 139:14)

To be "fearfully and wonderfully made" is another way of saying His design is "awesome" and "set apart with distinction."[15] God didn't mess up when He made you.

Your imperfections are not mistakes.

What we see as failures are the result of living in a world marred by sin (Romans 3:23; 8:18–25). We live as imperfect beings in a fallen world, and this manifests in obstacles, shortcomings, lifelong challenges, and incurable diseases or disabilities. It's not that God cursed people who have these issues. In His sovereign plan He is bringing forth redemption for all, even if we may not be able to comprehend it.

Though we can't always see God's goodness, it's always at work.

God designed you with purpose, even in the way you learn.

UNDERSTANDING LEARNING STYLES

Understanding different learning styles enhances not only the educational process but also lifelong learning. While no Bible verse (that I know of) confirms such a thing, I'm sure your own experiences and your observations of others have shown you the different ways people learn and process new information. Interestingly, these styles are debated within the fields of science, psychology, and education.[16] Still, I've seen enough evidence in myself, my family, and my clients to believe that we are definitely bent toward a particular way of learning.

The experts on learning styles have come up with dozens of combinations and descriptions, with the most common types being these:

1. *Auditory:* learning by hearing
   - easily comprehend oral instructions
   - tend to read instructions out loud
   - often hum when bored
2. *Visual:* learning by seeing
   - easily remember visual cues
   - tend to draw pictures and map information
   - often find busy places distracting
3. *Kinesthetic:* learning by doing, touching, and moving
   - easily remember by using hands and moving
   - tend to tap a foot or hand during times of learning
   - often need to take breaks from sitting for too long

As you think about what your own learning style might be, consider how it affects the outcomes of these activities:

- taking a permit test for your driver's license
- putting together a piece of furniture from a box kit
- assembling a child's toy on Christmas Eve
- following a recipe
- administering medication to a loved one
- participating in a Bible study
- filling out financial-aid forms for student loans

When I finally discovered that I was a visual and kinesthetic learner, I no longer felt strange about being the only one in the pew at church taking sermon notes. If I really want to absorb a message, I have to keep my pen moving, even if that means doodling a keyword. No, I'm not spacing out—I'm paying attention. It's the way God made me!

Determining your learning styles will help you understand the way God made you and how you can be the most effective student of life.

Friend, isn't it time to walk in light of the truth that God made you fearfully and wonderfully for a good purpose, even in the way you learn?

Trap and Transform

Discover Your Learning Style

Are you a "let me use my hands" type of woman? Can you listen to a lecture without fidgeting? Do you find it easier to remember things when they're color coded? These are just some of the clues to your learning styles. But rather than guessing, how about finding your learning style by using one of these assessments?

- HowToLearn.com Personal Learning Styles Quiz: www.howto learn.com/learning-styles-quiz
- EducationPlanner.org Self-Assessment: www.educationplanner .org/students/self-assessments/learning-styles.shtml
- Edutopia Assessment: www.edutopia.org/multiple -intelligences-assessment
- Highlands Ability Battery: www.elisapulliam.com/highlands[17]

Step 1: What Is Your Learning Style?

After completing one or more of the assessments, jot down your primary and secondary learning styles with reflections on how they each relate to your daily responsibilities.

1. _____

2. _____

Reflections

Step 2: What's the Impact?

1. How did your learning styles influence your educational experience?

2. How have your learning styles influenced your career choice and experience overall?

3. Now that you know your learning styles, how will you approach new opportunities in the future?

Go Deeper

1. How does uncovering your learning styles change the way you look back on your childhood experiences while also enabling a new way of thinking about yourself going forward?

2. How might your learning styles affect your current and future responsibilities?

3. What life-giving words do you need to hear God speak now about how He made you and your ability to learn?

𝓖ive It Over

Heavenly Father, thank You for making me unique, right down to the way I learn. Thank You that I'm fearfully and wonderfully made. Help me to know that fully! Please show me the relevancy of knowing my learning styles and applying that knowledge to my life. Help me to be a lifelong learner who uses her knowledge for Your purposes. In Jesus's name, amen. (Psalm 139:14)

The Pursuit of Purpose

Calling, Career, and Everything In-Between

For it is God who works in you to will and
to act in order to fulfill his good purpose.

—Philippians 2:13

We've spent the last few days looking at your internal wiring by discovering your personality, spiritual gifting, and learning styles. Now it's time to focus on the way your experiences have influenced your passions and sense of purpose, as they pertain to what many refer to as your *calling*. But first, we've got to settle what a *calling* is . . . and is not.

What Is a Calling?

As a life coach and mentor, I'm often asked for help on figuring out calling. It's as though finding your calling is the secret ingredient for having a meaningful, satisfying life. Equally so, not knowing your calling might mean you're wasting your life. But I don't think it is black and white, and I believe the focus on calling can actually be derailing. What do you think? Is knowing your calling important to understanding your purpose?

If you look up *calling* in the dictionary, you'll find that it refers to vocation, profession, or trade. Isn't it interesting that calling is about working, as in having a job for which you most likely get paid? (Unless you're a mom, which I consider a full-time, unpaid job.) Yet our cultural definition of *calling* focuses more on what we feel we were created or made to do—and most of us want both the *made to do* and *paid to do* to be the same thing. But is that realistic?

Maybe we have placed too much emphasis on calling and not enough focus on living fully right where we are.

Could this idea of having a calling (what we're made to do) and a matching career (what we're paid to do) be a cultural by-product that stems from the astronomical cost of higher education? Of course, I speak as a mother of teens, looking ahead to funding four years of college with the hopes that a paying job will result from the investment. Who would invest thousands of dollars without knowing the reason for doing so? Maybe the high price of a college degree is why there's so much emphasis on finding a career that not only provides income but also fulfills a life purpose. Did you know, however, that the average American Baby Boomer changes his or her job at least eleven times before retiring, with more than half of those jobs being held before age twenty-four?[18] Maybe those jobs reflect lateral moves within a career or whole new jobs. Regardless, it's unlikely that your job will be the same for a lifetime, so figuring out your calling—what you're made to do—and expecting it to be intertwined with a career is unlikely, even if that's what this generation of Millennials is after:

> Among Christians, there is an additional question: "What does God
> want me to do with my life?" According to Barna Group's study, only
> 40% of practicing Christians say they have a clear sense of God's calling
> on their lives. Christian Millennials are especially sensitive to this divine
> prompting—nearly half (48%) say they believe God is calling them to
> different work, yet they haven't yet made such a change.[19]

Maybe the answer isn't to make a job change. Maybe a job is supposed to pay the bills and you should experience what you're made to do some other way.

For years I felt called to impact teenagers, and I did so by making them welcome in my home. I started a ministry, and later a website, to help other moms impact their teens, but my paying job was as a graphic designer until I eventually became a life coach. Many of my life-coaching students feel called to become trained coaches themselves so that they can help other women, yet they continue to work as nurses, administrators, teachers, and stay-at-home moms. They are helping women at work and in life in general, but not in the way they feel called to. Some will continue their full-time jobs while coaching on the side. Others will eventually transition to full-time coaching as a business or a ministry. My point is this: finding a career that reflects your calling and a calling that you express in your career is a fluid process, because our jobs and our callings are ever changing around our circumstances, relationships, and responsibilities.

Pursue Purpose Instead

I do believe that the answer we're searching for isn't career or calling. It's really about life purpose.

We want to know what God has made us to do.

But what if purpose is about experiencing God working in you and through you in all your responsibilities and relationships?

> For it is God who works in you to will and to act in order to fulfill his good purpose. (Philippians 2:13)

Imagine if you defined your purpose through embracing this moment, this responsibility, this relationship, this circumstance with regard to God's bigger plans for your life. What if you found your purpose in simply enjoying all that He accomplishes through you every single day, not in the pursuit of something bigger, better, more meaningful? Wouldn't that free you up to simply be . . . and bring more creativity, flexibility, and passion into your life?

Think about it from this perspective: As you grow emotionally, physically, and intellectually, your abilities will change. As you mature spiritually, your desires change. As you experience the blessings and trials of life, even your priorities will change. If you are changing constantly, then your sense of life purpose should also be undergoing transformation. So rather than focusing on an outcome, what if you simply live for God in this moment as you find pleasure in doing this thing and the next thing with Him?

There is nothing wrong with wanting to be like Eric Liddell in *Chariots of Fire* and feel God's pleasure when you run . . . whatever that running may look like. Yet the truth is that Liddell ran as a world-renowned athlete for only a short time before heading to the mission field in China. Was it his calling to run fast—or to be a missionary? Or was it both, at different times in his life, because he was passionate about doing everything for the glory of God, whether he was running or spreading the gospel?

Finding What You're Made to Do

The secret in Eric Liddell's story is this: he felt God's pleasure when he ran fast because he was doing what he was made to do. So what is it that you're made to do? Forget calling. Let go of it being your career. Just think outside the box for a moment as you consider these questions:

- What fires you up?
- What can you do without ever running out of energy?
- Whom do you feel compelled to serve and help?
- What do you want to see changed in your community and the world?

Friend, the answers to these questions (which you'll have time to think about concretely later on) reveal the passions that have formed as a result of your God-given wiring and your life experiences.

Passions are an overflowing of who you are—you can't take them out of you!

Your passions may work into your career, or you may need to explore your passions outside your career. For example, your passion may be to write but instead you're busy changing dirty diapers and paying the bills. So you start a blog or keep a journal, simply because writing for you is like breathing. It has to happen.

Maybe your passion is to help homeless women find jobs, and so you volunteer at a shelter on the weekends while working in a human-resources department at a Fortune 500 company during the week. Your job is not your passion, but it pays the bills and frees you up to devote time to your passion after hours.

Passions are like fuel. They give you energy. They give you purpose. And they reflect the beauty of how God made you as well as how He wants to use you.

We can't ignore our passions, but we may have to get creative about how we tap into them. So how about pinpointing your passions by looking at what gives you God's pleasure and considering your purpose as you surrender your calling to the Lord?

Trap and Transform

Find Pleasure in His Purposes

Let's see how your wiring combined with your life experiences paint a picture of your passions and hint at the purpose God intends to accomplish through you.

Step 1: Pray and Reflect

Ask the Lord to clear your mind of distractions as you think back on your life.

1. From your childhood through present day, what events left a positive impact on you?

2. What events left a negative impact on you?

3. What relationships left a positive impact on you?

4. What relationships left a negative impact on you?

5. What accomplishments or awards have you received?

6. What did you enjoy doing as a child?

7. What do you enjoy devoting your free time to now?

8. What skills or talents did you develop as a child?

9. What skills or talents do you desire to develop now?

Step 2: If You Could Pick

Again, think back over your lifetime as you answer these questions.

1. With whom do you like to serve or work?

- Infants
- Elementary-school kids
- Middle-school kids
- High-school kids
- College kids
- Young adults
- Singles
- Marrieds
- Divorced folks
- Widowed folks
- The elderly
- Other: _____

2. What do you like to spend your time doing?
   - Administrating
   - Decorating
   - Leading
   - Managing finances
   - Offering hospitality
   - Organizing
   - Pursuing or teaching fitness
   - Serving
   - Studying nutrition and food
   - Other: _____

3. What issues get you fired up?
   - Abuse victims
   - Environment
   - Finances
   - Health
   - Marriage
   - Missions
   - Orphan care
   - Parenting
   - Social justice
   - Other: _____

Step 3: Put It Together

As you look over your answers and consider your life today, complete these statements:

1. I am passionate about serving this group of people:

2. I am passionate about meeting this need:

3. I am passionate about exploring this kind of work in the future, whether I do it as a job or in my nonwork hours:

Go Deeper

1. Have you focused on making your career your calling, or your calling your career? If so, what has been the result?

2. How would your life change if you harnessed your God-given passions as you sought God for His purposes?

3. How can you tap into your passions without changing your career?

ᎶGive It Over

Heavenly Father, thank You for working in me, accomplishing Your good purposes, even while I'm still figuring out what to do with my life. Help me see the passions You've cultivated in me and what they might reveal about my life purpose. Show me how You want to use me in this world. In Jesus's name, amen. (Philippians 2:13)

Phase 3

Overcome Obstacles

Remember, for all your adult life you'll be a woman. And how you live your life as a woman, all by yourself before God, is what makes the real you. Nothing on the exterior can touch or change that precious inner sanctuary—your heart, his dwelling place—unless you let it. And God, who loves you very much, has tailor made all your outer life—your circumstances, your relationships—to pressure you into becoming that beautiful woman he's planned for you to be.

—ANNE ORTLUND

A Mental Makeover

Understand Your Core Beliefs

For the word of God is alive and active.

—Hebrews 4:12

Well done, friend! You've made it halfway through this journey, and I hope you have a better sense of how God made you perfectly unique and on purpose. Now it's time to focus on what's standing in your way of becoming the woman God intended. Are you ready to put on your boxing gloves and knock down the obstacles keeping you from experiencing real life change?

The first one to tackle is your beliefs, which we've been doing throughout this journey, but now we'll consider the origin of your beliefs and how they line up with Scripture.

What Do You Believe?

Have you ever considered the beliefs you've "inherited" from your family and other influential people? Have you ever noticed the traditions and sayings that impact the way you do life? If you have a Christian heritage, are there certain church customs or often-quoted Bible passages that have shaped your lifestyle?

If you stopped to think about the beliefs *behind* your beliefs, you might see how deeply they influence the way you live and be surprised how much of what you thought was truth is not actually consistent with Scripture. Christian hip-hop artist Lecrae pointed this out in his powerfully delivered message to Liberty University students. He stated that only 10 percent of Christians see life through a biblical lens, 33 percent don't know that Isaiah is in the Old Testament, and 12 percent think Joan of Arc was Noah's wife.[20]

Does that make you laugh out loud, cringe, or wonder what you're missing? Let me explain. If 33 percent of Christians say they see life through the lens of Scripture but don't know that the book of Isaiah is in the Old Testament, and if 12 percent think Joan of Arc was Noah's wife, it seems Christians are not considering biblical truth at all. In their defense, maybe those beliefs were passed on to them and they never thought to verify those "facts" by searching the Scriptures.

I'll never forget my embarrassment when my husband gently pointed out what I thought was in Scripture was not a verse at all. I had no idea that "See no evil, hear no evil, speak no evil" was actually a Japanese proverb quoted in one of our daughter's beloved children's videos. That experience certainly made me think twice about other common sayings such as . . .

- "God won't ever give you more than you can handle."
- "If it is meant to be, then it will happen."
- "Life shouldn't be this hard."

Would you say these are paraphrases from the Bible? If you're stumped, don't fret—you're not alone. According to research from the Barna Group, most self-proclaimed Christ followers lack a Christian worldview.[21] Larry Osborne, author of *Ten Dumb Things Smart Christians Believe,* affirms the problem—too many Christians build their lives on misinterpretations of Scripture—but he also proposes a solution:

> Measure twice, cut once. . . . The same holds true for the spiritual principles
> upon which we base our life. Once we've made a decision or set a course
> of action, it's usually too late to go back and start checking out the accuracy
> of our assumptions.[22]

Osborne describes how knowing the truth as it's found in Scripture requires reading the verses in context and following the guidance of godly mentors:

Early in my faith journey I had some careful-thinking mentors who pointed out the folly of basing my belief system on what everybody else said rather than on careful biblical scrutiny. They taught me to avoid reading just my favorite verses. They showed me the importance of reading all the surrounding verses—and the rest of the book as well.

Their advice has served me well and saved me much heartache. It has also solidified my confidence in the Bible. The more I've learned to toss aside the clichés, happy talk, and cultural assumptions that don't fit with what the Bible actually says (or the way that life really works), the greater my trust in it as God's Word and the ultimate source of spiritual truth.[23]

Thy Word Is Truth

Oh yes, friend, it is wise to be instructed by those who know Scripture well, but we also need to dig into the Bible for ourselves in order to know and be guided by the truth. God designed the Word to be a tool for us to use every day.

For the word of God is alive and active. Sharper than any double-edged sword, it penetrates even to dividing soul and spirit, joints and marrow; it judges the thoughts and attitudes of the heart. (Hebrews 4:12)

When you spend time in Scripture, the Holy Spirit, who dwells in every believer, draws upon the truths you've learned from the Word and brings them to mind when you need to act on your beliefs:

The Advocate, the Holy Spirit, whom the Father will send in my name, will teach you all things and will remind you of everything I have said to you. (John 14:26)

By cultivating this well of wisdom, you'll avoid conforming to the patterns of this world and be able to take captive your thoughts and make them obedient to Christ (Romans 12:2; 2 Corinthians 10:5). This is critical because the enemy of God, Satan, is continually attacking you with his lies. Scripture calls the devil the "father of lies" (John 8:44), who wants to wear you down with one onslaught after another. He does battle in your mind not only with lies but with questions that cause you to doubt God. It's the same game he played with Eve in the garden, asking one life-altering, doubt-producing question: "Did God really say . . . ?" (Genesis 3:1). And with that, Eve was off and running into forbidden territory instead of standing on the truth. If only she had told him off and clung to what she knew God had said.

Unfortunately, the way of Eve is the path we often take.

Is it any surprise that we doubt God's promise and forsake His wisdom as easily as Eve did? We give in to our feelings, especially in the face of opposition, trials, and exhaustion. That's exactly what happened with my middle daughter, Abby, when she was only thirteen (yes, the Enemy likes to get us doubting God when we're young). All I did was ask her, "Are you really going to wear *that* out of the house?" I know that's the equivalent of declaring war on a teenage soul. I should have chosen my words more carefully, but I couldn't hit rewind. As I feared, Abby didn't hear my sincerity or concern. She reacted based on how she felt rather than on recognizing my intentions. Aren't we all guilty of doing this?

By God's grace, I was able to see past her response and into what was happening in her heart and mind. See, my precious Abby was mad, but the real issue wasn't with me or her clothing. She was still grieving the death of a classmate—a process that takes any human being on an emotional roller coaster. A fire was burning in her thought life, and my little question about clothing was like throwing on another large log.

Has this happened to you, when something you're feeling isn't yet processed and a trigger sets your emotions ablaze?

So there she stood, eye to eye with me, doubting my intentions in the same way Eve doubted God's best. When I challenged her to tell me if she really thought how she felt was based on the truth, she said the truest thing of all.

"I don't know what is true. I only know what I feel."

Between Satan's antics and our own intense feelings, the truth is often clouded.

It takes a disciplined mind to choose the truth over feelings, and it takes diligence to ward off the lies that seep into your soul.

Your thoughts will run all over if you don't guard them, because it's easier to believe the lies . . . lies about what you need in order to feel good and how you should look in order to be accepted. Lies about how you should clean your house or spend your money. Lies about what a Christian marriage should look like and how you should educate your kids. Oh yes, it's possible to build your life on a series of lies, even when your heart is completely devoted to God.

Friend, your beliefs impact how you live, and they impact what you teach to the next generation. So how about doing a mental makeover as you move toward meeting the new you?

Trap and Transform

Do a Mental Makeover

Determining whether your thoughts are in line with the truth is an ongoing process. It starts by listening to the words you say, because "the mouth speaks what the heart is full of" (Matthew 12:34). Your words are really confessions of the heart, much like leaks from the CIA on matters of national intelligence, although you don't need to be a professional investigator to figure out what they mean. You can also determine what you believe by considering common belief statements while digging into Scripture to see if they are true.

Step 1: "Is It True?" Quiz

Would you say these statements are biblically accurate? Write *yes* or *no*.

1. _____ God helps those who help themselves.

2. _____ Money is the root of all evil.

3. _____ To thine own self be true.

4. _____ God works in mysterious ways.

5. _____ Pride comes before the fall.

6. _____ God will not give you more than you can handle.

7. _____ You should follow your heart.

8. _____ This too shall pass.

9. _____ All things work together for good.

10. _____ Spare the rod, spoil the child.

It might seem that most of these statements are biblically accurate—they are in the Bible, after all—right? But even though we may find verses that appear to support these ideas, they are skewed. That's because these statements are misquotes of Scripture. Each one picks keywords to prove a point but misses the context entirely. Take time to look up the verses to see the *whole* Scripture truth:

(1) Romans 5:6, 8 (2) 1 Timothy 6:10 (3) none (4) Deuteronomy 29:29 (5) Proverbs 16:18 (6) 1 Corinthians 10:13 (7) Proverbs 3:5–6 (8) none (9) Romans 8:28 (10) Proverbs 13:24

Step 2: Which Lies Do You Believe?

Read through these statements, then circle the ones you believe. When you're finished, look up the Scripture references to see if that statement reflects the truth. If you can't figure it out, there's help for you below.

1. If only I were perfect . . . (Psalm 18:30; Romans 3:22–23; Philippians 3:12; 1 John 1:8)
2. If I try hard enough, they'll like me. (Galatians 1:10; Colossians 3:23–24)
3. God wants me to be happy. (Acts 20:22–24; Philippians 4:11–14; James 1:2–3)
4. My worth is found in what I do. (Psalm 139:13–14; Romans 12:3)
5. Life shouldn't be this hard. (Matthew 6:34; John 16:33; Philippians 3:13–14)
6. I'm a good person. (Jeremiah 17:9; Matthew 15:19; Romans 3:10–12)
7. If I am good, then God will love me and life won't be hard. (John 3:16; 8:1–11; 16:33; Romans 5:8; Ephesians 2:8–9; 1 Peter 4:12–13)
8. If I'm really a Christian, then I should never be angry or depressed. (Mark 11:15–16; 14:32–34; John 11:33–35)
9. If this relationship was meant to be, it wouldn't be this hard. (1 Corinthians 7:28; Hebrews 12:14)
10. I need to forgive myself. (Psalm 32:1; Matthew 6:12; 26:28)

Here are the truthful, biblical statements that the listed verses reflect. As you read through them, circle the ones you would like to memorize. Look up the correlating verses and write them out on index cards.

1. Christ is perfect.
2. I am approved by God.
3. God isn't concerned with happiness but wholeness.
4. My worth is found in whose I am—and I belong to the Lord.
5. God promises that in this life we will have problems.
6. No one is good. Not one.
7. God's love is unconditional and given to me freely, but that doesn't mean I won't experience suffering.
8. Salvation doesn't change our emotions.
9. Relationships are hard, and we have to work together to resolve conflicts.
10. You can't pay for your own debts or forgive your own sins, but you can receive God's forgiveness.

Go Deeper

1. What inherited beliefs have shaped your identity and the way you're living? Is that good, bad, neither?

2. How often do you allow your emotions to trump the truth? What could you do to counteract this reaction?

3. Would you say your beliefs are consistent with biblical truth? If not, what would you like to do about it?

Give It Over

God, thank You for making it so plain in Your Word that what I think impacts how I live. Forgive me for not being careful about what I choose to believe and for unknowingly living according to traditions, sayings, and in some cases, lies. Please set me free from any and all beliefs that are not formed by Your truth. In Jesus's name, amen. (John 8:44; Romans 12:2; Hebrews 4:12)

A Values-Driven Life

Reshape Your Core Values

...follow the example of Christ.

—1 CORINTHIANS 11:1

As we continue this journey of uncovering the obstacles standing in the way of real life change, I want to introduce you to the concept of core values. Values set your life in motion, impacting your lifestyle choices, the way you engage in relationships, how you use your resources, and what you choose to do with your time.

While core beliefs reflect the foundational truths influencing how you respond to life, core values reflect personal preferences, family traditions, and cultural habits that affect how you live your life.

For example, a core value might be something like "People are more important than things." Maybe you learned that from your mom or an aunt. If that value guides your decision making, you'll quickly drop everything for a friend in need or for a social occasion. In contrast, if one of your core values is "A finished list reflects a good day's work," you might dismiss that friend in need so that you can get everything done that you planned to do.

As you mature, grow, and experience life from new vantage points, you'll experience the power struggle among your values. They will often be in conflict, internally and externally, and you have to choose which value will prevail. More importantly, as you draw closer to the Lord and immerse yourself in the Word, it will be impossible for your values to remain unchanged! They should conform more and more to biblical values.

So how do you know what your values are? And which ones need to conform to biblical truth? That's what you're about to find out.

Caught and Taught and Competing

Your *values* are so deeply rooted in your *belief system* that you may not even know what they are—they may feel one and the same. In my own life, I held the value that "financial prosperity was evidence of success," and I also believed that "I need to live a certain way in order to be happy." This was the result of my beliefs and values having been significantly shaped during my middle-school years as my family went from doing without to living it up, thanks to a surge in my dad's financial success. I not only liked the new lifestyle, but I also expected it to be my norm for the rest of my life.

Oh, the irony that God gave me a husband who feels passionately called to teach in a Christian school, which is not a high-paying field. In addition, we've shared the value of my being a work-at-home mom. As a result, I've had to surrender my fancy lifestyle expectations and embrace a budget-conscious way of living. The transition was not without a struggle as I came to terms with my real life and gave up the one I thought I needed! While a trip to Hawaii might be lovely, my values have adjusted so much that I can be just as happy packing up our family for a weekend of low-budget togetherness.

I share this story with you to illustrate these four truths about values:

1. Values are formed through life experiences.
2. Values impact life choices.
3. Values will sometimes compete internally and externally.
4. Values can, and oftentimes should, change.

Your values are caught and taught throughout your life as you watch, listen, and respond to what was modeled by those around you, especially as a young person under the mentorship of parents, extended family members, teachers, and coaches. Many of your values-driven decisions are linked to your own family's traditions, as well as by ethnic and cultural norms.

I'll never forget the few meals we experienced at my great-aunt Tillie's home shortly after moving back East from the Midwest, where we had no family nearby. It was a cultural shock to sit at a twelve-foot-long table covered with food from one end to the other. Just as we finished what should have been the main dish, five more courses followed. It's an Italian thing to value food to such a great degree—it's a representation of love, so there's a lot of it to go around. For the remainder of my adolescent years, family gatherings meant an incredible selection of Italian delicacies. You can imagine the conflict I felt internally when I celebrated my first holiday as a married woman. Stephen's family, with their German heritage and post–Depression era traditions, places a distinct value on frugality. They serve good food in moderation, with an emphasis on utilizing whatever meat and produce are on sale. It's quite the contrast to my Italian family. Neither way is right nor wrong, but both reflect values.

It's human nature to adopt values on everything from food to how to decorate a home to how often one should exercise to what it means to live an eco-friendly lifestyle. Our values influence where we go to church and what type of job we believe is worth taking. We have values regarding when to get married and how many children to have. Values are everywhere!

Values are often the silent partner guiding your decision making.

Well, they're silent until an internal or external conflict arises, such as when the value of family time competes with the value of providing an income. Or when the value of a luxurious vacation competes with the value of sticking with a budget. How about when the value of staying fit competes with the value of working late?

These value conflicts often lead to a feeling of being stuck or trapped.

The best way to deal with competing values is to identify what they are and then look at how they line up with the Word of God. As believers, our values should be biblically sound and also follow the example of Christ. By looking to see how Jesus lived and what He taught, we can learn biblical values about relationships, responsibilities, resources, and reactions. The apostle Paul stated this principle quite simply:

Follow my example, as I follow the example of Christ. (1 Corinthians 11:1)

Jesus was about His Father's business, so there is no better example for us to follow. For example, what did Jesus say about finances and friendship, time management and priorities, serving others and being served? What is the importance of feeding the poor and providing for orphans? How should you embrace a single mom or reach out to an elderly neighbor? When the Word, in particular Christ's example, shapes your values, the way you live will change. Your life will no longer be centered on what you feel or prefer, but rather you'll find yourself asking, *What does God have to say about this?*

Are you ready to identify your values and begin looking at them through the lens of Scripture? This one step can bring such clarity to how you live.

Trap and Transform

The Shaping of Your Values

Values influence your life, so why not choose to intentionally shape your values? By taking the time to pinpoint your values, you'll actually find the solutions to these three common problems:

1. Discover the reasons why you feel stuck in a particular area of life or in a relationship, because of a core-value conflict.
2. Determine why you feel out of step with God, because your values are not lining up with biblical values.
3. Define the priorities shaped by your values and redefine those that don't line up with biblical values.

Remember, your values can and should change as you mature, especially in your faith, so embrace this process with an eagerness to see your life from a fresh perspective.

Step 1: Consider Your Values

Below you'll find a list of words that represent typical core values. Look over the list, then circle the words or phrases that resonate with you the most. If there's a word or phrase that comes to mind that is not on the list, feel free to add it.

Accomplishment	Freedom
Approval	Frugality
Artistic	Fulfillment
Authenticity	Fun
Beauty	Gentleness
Biblical truth	Genuineness
Boldness	Grace
Boundaries	Growth
Career	Health
Carefulness	Honesty
Cleanliness	Hope
Communication	Humility
Community	Humor
Compassion	Independence
Competence	Influence
Competition	Integrity
Confidence	Joy
Consistency	Justice
Control	Learning
Creativity	Love
Determination	Loyalty
Diligence	Marriage
Discipline	Mentoring
Drama	Moderation
Efficiency	Money
Elegance	Music
Encouragement	Nurturing
Excellence	Obedience
Excitement	Orderliness
Faithfulness	Patience
Family	Peace
Fitness	Perfection
Forgiveness	Performance

Persistence	Solitude
Productivity	Spiritual growth
Purity	Stability
Quality	Success
Recognition	Tech savvy
Relaxation	Technology
Sanctification	Tolerance
Security	Trust
Self-control	Truth
Self-esteem	Worship
Sensitivity	Other: _____
Service	Other: _____
Silence	Other: _____
Simplistic	Other: _____
Sincerity	Other: _____

Step 2: Reflect on Your Values

1. Can you identify the core values you inherited from your parents or other significant adults in your life?

2. Can you identify the core values that are a direct result of what you've experienced in your own life?

3. Do your core-value words resonate with biblical principles? If so, indicate the verses that come to mind. (You can use BibleGateway .com if you need to search keywords.)

Step 3: Choose Your Values and Consider Their Impact

Looking over your list, pick the top four you believe describe your core values currently and/or the ones you want to be prevalent in your life. Write those words below, together with a statement that reflects what each value means to you. If possible, include the Bible reference that expresses that value.

1.

2.

3.

4.

Go Deeper

1. Did you experience an "aha" moment in discovering your core values? If so, describe it.

2. Which of your values needs adjustment in order line up with biblical truth? Describe what steps you will take in that direction.

3. In what ways have your core values influenced your relationships, reactions, resources, and responsibilities? Describe the positive and negative outcomes, then think about what you'd like to happen going forward.

Give It Over

Lord God, thank You for the good influences on my life and the way they've shaped my values. Please show me how Christ's example is relevant to everyday decision making and life choices, especially in terms of my values. Change my thinking about my priorities to line up with Your truth as I embrace the relationships and responsibilities You've given me. In Jesus's name, amen. (1 Corinthians 11:1)

Break Free

Get Out of the Comparison Trap

Don't compare yourself with others.

—GALATIANS 6:4, MSG

Isn't it amazing how easily we can find someone with whom we can compare ourselves? It feels like a default response to focus on the good in someone else's life, then give up enjoying the good in ours. Maybe that's why it is said that comparison is the thief of joy. And we know who the thief really is—the devil himself.

The Enemy erodes joy with a comparison game of should-haves, could-haves, and would-haves.

Of course, his work may not be obvious. Consider how easily you fall into a pattern of thinking along these lines:

- *I would be so much more confident if I were as skinny as she is.*
- *If he made as much money as my cousin, then we could finally get married and buy a house.*
- *I know I should have gotten that other degree, then I would be happy like my boss.*

When thoughts like these start swirling in your mind and heart, it's a telltale sign that the comparison trap is threatening to snatch you up. So what should you do? Develop a game plan for avoiding the snare of comparison. It's possible, friend. With a little work and some strategizing, you'll be set free to live the life God is calling you to . . . with much more joy. I know, because I was once trapped in the ugly game of comparison and learned (in a rather humble-pie sort of way) how to embrace the life God gave me.

THE UGLINESS OF COMPARISON

When I was a young momma of two little girls, I was over at my friend Suzy's house, doing my best to listen intently to her and not be distracted by the chatter of our girls playing nearby. We were catching up on life and sharing future dreams when she pulled out a Christmas card from a friend who happened to be on a wild faith journey. As Suzy described the play-by-play, I couldn't believe the way my heart twisted between awe and jealousy. On the one hand, I was excited for the way God was expanding this woman's territories and fulfilling her life dreams, but I also wondered, *What about me, Lord?*

Fast-forward a few years. That question had continued to chisel away at my soul, especially as I watched the friend's ministry explode across the Internet. When the opportunity arose to enter a blog-writing competition to win a ticket to her conference, I jumped at the chance. I was longing for the training and kindred connections that the conference would provide. I felt certain that's what God wanted for me too.

Well, it was not His plan. And I didn't like it one bit. With bitterness in my heart, I gave up the dream and turned back to my "real life," which meant heading to Target for my weekly shopping trip. I never expected to bump into my best friend as I rounded the clearance end cap. Before I could even say hello, Andrea asked what was wrong. That's because friends like her can read my heart on my sleeve. Not bothering with an excuse, I gave her the honest reason: "I didn't win the scholarship."

She knew exactly what I was talking about, and before I could even get another word out, she spoke truth to my soul:

"God is going to do in you what He is going to do in you, and it's not going to be like what He is doing in someone else."

Yes, my friend, God's plans for me or for you won't look like His plans for anyone else. And I think it's time we get our minds around that fact—even if it's hard.

Embrace It or Lose It

Have you struggled with wanting what someone else has or has accomplished? Do you wish God would work in your life the way you see Him work in the lives of others? You're not alone in your desires to want what seems good, but have you ever thought about the good you'd have to give up in order to get it?

In pining away for someone else's story, you might be missing the one He is writing in your life.

He's been busy writing His purposes through His people since the beginning of time. Will you take up your part instead of wishing for someone else's?

- There was only one Moses who saw God in a burning bush (Exodus 3).
- There was only one Gideon leading an army into battle outnumbered four hundred to one (Judges 6–7).
- There was only one Mary chosen to give life to the Savior of this world (Luke 1).
- There was only one Paul who went from persecutor to proclaimer of the truth (Acts 9).
- There was only one Peter who denied his Lord but later became the rock on which the church was built (John 18; Matthew 16:18).

God, who took nobodies and made them somebodies, longs to do something freshly amazing in you.

There is only one you.

There is only one me.

Both of us are unique.

Both of us have distinct purposes.

God doesn't hand out duplicate scripts. Each one of us is chosen to play a specialized part in the story He is writing.

As I've said before, you are chosen by God, friend (1 Peter 2:9). Yes, it's worth emphasizing, because believing this one truth can change your life. You are not overlooked, nor are you too much, not enough, or worth less than anyone else. You are not "as is" or stuck forever. You are not what others say about you. You are more than what others neglect to say about you. You are a beloved child of God, a handpicked instrument by which He longs to accomplish His work in and through. Embracing this truth is the antidote to envy, greed, jealousy, insecurity, and discontentment. It frees you to live the life God has given to you, sharing with others what you know of Him, see in Him, and experience because of Him.

You are a key part of a timeless story meant to reveal the glory of God.

When you compare your story to other people's, wanting what they have, you're really saying your story is not good enough. In those moments, when your heart is steeped in discontentment instead of gratefulness, you're giving up the abundantly full life God designed for you (John 10:10). Maybe you feel justified, especially if your current situation is awful. But the fact is that for anything good you see in someone else's life, you can bet there is an equal measure of bad. The rain falls on all of us. So when comparison rears its green ugly head, use it to your advantage, my friend. Let that feeling of despair become your sounding alarm to escape the trap of comparison.

The Choice of Focus

Are you ready to practice getting out of the comparison trap through embracing a posture change that ushers in a heart change? Take your hands, put them under your chin, and push your face upward. Are you looking straight up? Great! Now you're ready to break free and focus entirely on God's purposes for you.

The only way out of the comparison trap is through shifting your attention from outward to upward.

This isn't just a physical shift—it must be a heart, mind, and soul shift to focus on God's purposes instead of paying attention to what everyone else has, does, and pursues. It requires an intentional inventory of the person God made you to be and the work He's given you to do:

> Make a careful exploration of who you are and the work you have
> been given, and then sink yourself into that. Don't be impressed with
> yourself. Don't compare yourself with others. Each of you must take
> responsibility for doing the creative best you can with your own life.
> (Galatians 6:4–5, MSG)

However, just focusing on God won't make jealousy go away. You also need to tell God you feel "less than" and invite Him to fill you with His truth. The sooner you get honest, the better off you'll be because a simple case of insecurity leads to jealousy, which gives way to gossip, slander, and more. Should we be surprised that Scripture warns us of this?

> For I am afraid that when I come I may not find you as I want you to be, and you may not find me as you want me to be. I fear that there may be discord, jealousy, fits of rage, selfish ambition, slander, gossip, arrogance and disorder. (2 Corinthians 12:20)

By God's grace, I finally came to terms with the fact that my unbridled feelings of jealousy gave way to sin as I harbored envious thoughts about my sister in Christ. I also realized I needed to confess my sin before God and seek His forgiveness. As I sat raw with emotion before God, I felt relief from the burden of jealousy and was compelled to apologize to that woman I had envied.

This woman hadn't even known my feelings toward her, so why should I say something? Maybe I felt it was the right thing to do since we had actually spent time together when she was a speaker at my church's women's retreat and we had once shared a dinner at a friend's home. While I could have reconciled it all before the Lord, I felt I should also apologize to her, so I sent off an e-mail later that day, not sure it would even get through.

A few days later, I was tossing and turning during a nap when the phone rang. The caller ID announced something that sounded like "Eesa Urqurst," and on the very last ring, I realized it was Lysa. Yes, Lysa TerKeurst, the *New York Times* best-selling author and founder of Proverbs 31 Ministries, long before she became widely known. She had received my e-mail and felt compelled to reach out to me. We chatted for a good long bit, and her words resonated with that same poignant truth my friend Andrea said months earlier:

We need to live the stories God is writing in our lives.

For me, that story was all about being home with my littles and serving from the overflow of God in me, right in the community He planted me in. It wasn't time to jaunt off to conferences, pursue writing more intentionally, or launch a ministry—as much as those desires burned inside of me. It was time to accept the life God gave me instead of wanting someone else's story to be mine.

Friend, what step do you need to take to get out of the comparison trap and live the life God intended for you?

Trap and Transform

Get Out of the Trap

Are you ready to figure out how to get free of the comparison trap? It starts with figuring out what triggers cause you to land there in the first place. By discovering how to respond to them with the truth, you'll be able to steer clear of the trap through focusing your attention on the Lord.

Step 1: What Are Your Comparison Triggers?

Check off the issues that cause you to compare yourself to others:

❑ Artistic ability
❑ Athletic ability
❑ Body weight
❑ Children
❑ Credentials
❑ Degrees
❑ Experiences
❑ Extended families
❑ Families
❑ Fashion
❑ Hair
❑ House size

❑ House style
❑ Income level
❑ Jobs
❑ Leadership positions
❑ Ministries
❑ Musical ability
❑ Schools
❑ Skin type
❑ Spouses
❑ Vacations
❑ Other: _____
❑ Other: _____

Step 2: What Are Your "If Only" Statements?

For example, if your body image or weight is a common trigger, do you find yourself saying, "If only I were as skinny as Tiffany, I know I would feel better about myself"? Write down your top three triggers and the "if only" statements you typically use.

1. Trigger:

   If only . . .

2. Trigger:

   If only . . .

3. Trigger:

   If only . . .

Step 3: What's the Truth?

As you consider those triggers and correlating "if only" statements, can you think of a Bible verse that trumps each feeling with the truth? If so, write those verses below. If not, use this time to pray and seek God for His perspective.

Go Deeper

1. What good things do you see God doing in your life that are totally unique to your story?

2. What causes you to fall into the comparison trap most often? What can you do to avoid it in the future?

3. If jealousy has marked your life, will you confess it to the Lord and
reconcile any relationships that have been broken as a result of that sin?

Give It Over

*Lord, I want out of the comparison trap once and for all. Help me
to see my triggers and defeat them with Your truth. Reveal to me the
ways You're accomplishing Your purposes in my life. Lead me to a
place of contentment as I let You work in my life. In Jesus's name,
amen. (1 Corinthians 3:3; Galatians 6:4–5)*

Let It Go

Crush Your Idols

They exchanged the truth about God
for a lie, and worshiped and served
created things rather than the Creator.

—Romans 1:25

I dolatry is one of those rarely spoken of, easily ignored issues, but it could be the one thing holding you back from meeting the new you. It's quite possible that you're worshiping a small-*g* god instead of living for the One who made you. And if that is the case, you're missing out on the life He intended for you. How can you know if idolatry is one of your obstacles? By carefully considering the state of your heart and seeing what is truly getting the majority of your time and attention.

AN UNLIKELY, LIFE-CHANGING APPOINTMENT

I suppose it's not every day that you get a recommendation about a great sermon series from your hairdresser, but apparently this was a divine appointment designed to do more than cover my gray. Danielle had recently finished listening to Pastor Brad Bigney's "Gospel Treason" series about idolatry, and she was brimming with insight on how idols are an everyday issue for us modern folk.[24]

I always thought *idolatry* meant worshiping something like a golden calf or a bronze statue, and I never thought of it in any other form. But idolatry is really any type of excessive devotion, adoration, obsession, or reverence toward someone or something that is not God. Hmm. Wouldn't you agree that we can be excessive in our adoration of technology and status? That we often have unhealthy devotion toward people and pursuits? That we are capable of revering our reputation and academic accolades?

When you give something or someone else the attention God deserves, that's idolatry.

Stop and consider what you devote your time and energies to. In other words, where is God on your to-do list? What else makes up that list? Is it the insistence that all the children have matching outfits for the family picture, which takes weeks of planning? Is it getting the project turned in to your boss early, with all the bells and whistles, causing you to miss your daughter's softball game? Is it running the Mother's Day Tea better than the former committee chair did, even if it means you spend more time at church than you do at home in the weeks leading up to it?

Idolatry is a deeply invasive issue, burrowing itself behind masks and winding its way around excuses, because on the surface the mission seems reasonable.

It's fine to work on a to-do list or to put forth extra effort on a project for work. It's a good idea to plan a nice family picture or a lovely tea. But at what cost? For what purpose? What's motivating your actions? Is it a desire to glorify God or to make yourself look good?

At the heart of idolatry is one solitary problem—one that Paul called out and is still alive today:

They exchanged the truth about God for a lie, and worshiped and
served created things rather than the Creator—who is forever praised.
(Romans 1:25)

What are you worshiping instead of God? Whom are you serving instead of the Creator?

BUSY, NOT BEST

Maybe you are living the way I was, so busy doing things for God that you forget about Him in the process. Throughout my twenties and well into my thirties, I got involved in ministry because I really wanted to use my talents and abilities for the glory of God. Initially, it was through serving as a youth leader at my church and then taking on mentoring relationships with the teens around me (at the time, my husband was a teacher at a boarding school, so there were hundreds of girls eager to be loved and guided). Investing in them came from a pure desire to see them not make the same mistakes I did and to encourage them to live for the Lord.

However, somewhere along the way, my need to please and to prove my worth skewed my pursuits. Ironically, it was about the same time blogging became popular, and I began writing for the public eye. Instead of simply serving the Lord from the overflow, my work became all about the stats—all those hits, Likes, and Shares stole my attention. I could no longer write a devotion about mentoring without it being about changing the world in six hundred words. Having a meaningful relationship with a broken young woman wasn't significant enough, as now I wanted to reach hundreds of women like her. While those desires were not wrong, the motive of my heart was not fully pure—I wanted to be seen and known more than I wanted God to be glorified. Of course, I didn't realize it at the time. The "aha" moment happened when the Holy Spirit revealed to me that my focus was more on what I could accomplish than it was on working alongside God. I was all about my timetable and agenda instead of the Lord's, as Sarah Young points out in *Jesus Calling:* "I, the Creator of the universe, have deigned to cocreate with you. Do not try to hurry this process."[25]

I was working toward a bigger audience, a broader platform, a more significant ministry (according to the world's standards), and anything that stood in my way really set me off. That was the clue that made me realize there was a problem. I complained endlessly about the chores, even though I said caring for my home was a priority. My kids were forever hearing me say "One more minute," when it would really take me one more hour to accomplish all that I thought I had to do and I couldn't let it go unfinished. And my desire to invest in the unseen opportunities to serve waned, while I got caught up in the increasing demands of marketing and platform growth.

Even though I said I was living for Jesus Christ, I was actually serving another triune god: me, myself, and I. It was all about my accomplishments and completions. Praises and approvals. Plans and purposes.

What about you? What's your idol? You'll have to look closely, because "idolatry flies under the radar."[26] Is it your job or hobby? Is it your role as a wife or mom? Is it your mission to live green or to serve the underprivileged? Is it possible that a good thing has turned idolatrous for you? As Bigney describes it, your idolatry lies in your "functional god"—*that thing* or *that person* dictating your behavior and falsely filling your needs.[27] And yet that very idol breaks down your relationship with the Most High God and keeps His transforming work from fully manifesting in you. That's because idolatry is a sin, and we sin in order to keep our idols alive. We think we need them, because to set them aside requires trusting God at a whole new level.

An idol's grip makes it feel impossible to just let it go.

God does not necessarily want us to stop what we're doing, but He does want to be first and foremost in our hearts. It's our focus that matters. He wants a pure relationship with us, deeply rooted in worshiping Him, the very One who made us to live and move and find our purpose in this world (Acts 17:24–25).

In order to keep from idolatry, you have to identify the underlying god dictating your decisions and commanding your emotions (Psalm 106:36). You can often see a clue when the object of worship is removed. There's a sense of loss, ensuing anger, bartering, sadness, and denial, before coming to acceptance. That's the crushing of an idol, and it's a good thing, even though it's painful.

Consider how you might feel if the reputation you worked so hard to keep above reproach was crushed by gossip. Or what if a house flip, which took all your money, turned into a house flop? What if all that time you spent preparing for a marathon ended in an injury that kept you from participating? None of these pursuits—a reputation, a house renovation, or training for a race—is idolatrous, but idolatry occurs when the outcome becomes more important than anything else in your life—especially God. That's how you know there's a problem in your heart: your pursuit of a good thing has trumped your devotion to the Lord and your pliability in His hands.

So what should you do when idolatry has gotten the best of you? Confess, my friend. Tell God what's going on inside of you, and ask Him to set your heart and focus straight. Be on guard: don't let anything become more important than the Lord and joining Him in His work. Loosen the grip on your must-haves and must-dos, and free yourself to live within His precious will.

Trap and Transform

Crush Your Idols

In these steps, you'll have an opportunity to reflect on whether idolatry has woven itself into your life. Once you discover your idols, I'll guide you in seeking God for a heart transformation.

Step 1: What Is Consuming Your Time, Resources, and Mental Focus?

Take time to consider all you do in a given week. Make a list of your responsibilities, then jot down how much time, money, and focus you spend on each.

Step 2: Where Are Your Idols Hiding?

Looking at your answers in Step 1, can you name some of your idols? Remember, your idols may look like people, things, or even attributes or opportunities you wish you had. If you're sinning in order to pursue them, those are idols too. Group them accordingly:

People:

Things:

Attributes (like reputation):

Opportunities and plans:

Step 3: How Can You Crush Your Idols?

What action steps might you need to take to break the stronghold of your idols? For example, if blogging is your idol, do you need to take time off or establish new boundaries? If your career is your idol, do you need to start volunteering in your community in order to take the focus off work? If mothering is your idol, do you need to find ways to shift the focus off an unhealthy obsession with being a mom by using your gifts and talents in other ways? As you think of your idols, seek the Lord for His leading and confess to Him what you feel. Also search the Scriptures to find key verses that speak to each issue. Write them down, then memorize them.

Go Deeper

1. How does this concept of idolatry strike you? Is it a new concept? A familiar and timely reminder?

2. Do you have any idols? If so, what are you going to do about them?

3. Who can hold you accountable in this idol-crushing process?

Give It Over

Heavenly Father, thank You for revealing the idolatry in my life. Show me, God, how to crush my idols and walk this road of repentance humbly before You as I reprioritize my life according to Your Word. May I learn how to worship You alone, my Creator and God. In Jesus's name, amen. (Proverbs 4:23; Romans 1:25; 1 John 5:21)

Unchained

Walk in Forgiveness

Be kind and compassionate to one
another, forgiving each other, just as
in Christ God forgave you.

—EPHESIANS 4:32

I'd love to say you're all done with the hard part of this obstacle-demolishing week, but there's still one more worth tackling. It's actually both an obstacle and a solution in the journey of meeting the new you. It's the matter of forgiveness . . . or more accurately, unforgiveness.

FORGIVENESS FREES US FROM THE CHAINS OF PAIN

Why is it that we resist the process of forgiveness? Do we avoid it because pride gets the best of us and fear makes the worst of us? Are we afraid to admit we're angry and hurting? Maybe we've been duped into believing the lie that if we let go of the anger, we might get hurt again. Yet choosing to hold on to hurt—choosing not to forgive—leads to that pain becoming part of us. It is only through forgiving others that we become unchained and able to really move on.

Have you bought into the mind-set that forgiving means forgetting? Well, it's not true!

Forgiving is not the same as forgetting. Forgiving is about remembering and releasing.

The act of forgiveness requires a bold recognition of a wound, an offense, or a sin committed or inflicted, either intentionally or accidentally. Yes, forgiveness most definitely involves remembering because that is the only way to release the hurt and trust God with the outcome. Forgiveness is the beginning of the healing process.

Choosing to forgive is like snipping hundreds of wires connected to the bomb hidden within your heart.

Oh yes. You might know those wires as well as I do—wires that represent bitterness, rage, and resentment. Wires woven tightly together with memories of shame, betrayal, and guilt. Wires that produce sparks as they rub against one another and injure innocent bystanders with critical words and cutting insults.

Unforgiveness wires our soul to the past yet causes explosions in the present.

That's what happens when we hold on to the pain and bury it inside instead of owning it and releasing it to God. Of course, we often don't know that's what we're doing. We think we're just moving on. Maybe that's why God says to rid ourselves of it—all that ugliness—through choosing to forgive:

> Get rid of all bitterness, rage and anger, brawling and slander, along with
> every form of malice. Be kind and compassionate to one another, forgiving
> each other, just as in Christ God forgave you. (Ephesians 4:31–32)

Forgiveness is not setting the offender free—as in letting him or her off the hook—but trusting God to put the person on His hook. Think about that for a minute. What if you let go of the offender and the punishment you think he or she deserves and instead choose to respond in faith: *Hey, God, here's this person who hurt me. Do as You please. I trust Your decision more than mine.* God is the fairest of all judges, so who better to determine the consequence or pardon the offense?

That was the question I chose to wrestle with as I began to see how my unforgiveness toward my parents was an obstacle in my life.

BECOMING UNCHAINED

Isn't it amazing that the ones we love most are often the ones we need to forgive most? Maybe it's human nature to hurt those closest to you, even if that hurt was never intended. I'm certain that was the case with my parents, because I know they wholly, fully love me as I do them. I believe they had my best interests in mind, but unfortunately, their wounds from dysfunctional childhoods and life's disappointments—as well as the strain of a difficult marriage created by financial challenges, major relocations, and job issues—overflowed onto me. That pain caused me to harbor bitterness toward them, which was an obstacle in our relationship and stole joy from my life every single day.

The problem was that I didn't know how to forgive them because I felt guilty for even being mad in the first place. Have you felt this way too? Maybe about a parent or spouse, or about a friend or distant relative?

I also wrestled with this matter of forgiveness because as a Christian I didn't think I had the right to be angry. Further, as I compared my life to others', I wondered if I had a real reason to be angry. *My childhood really wasn't that bad. Who am I to be so bitter?* Plus, as a thirty-something momma watching her own kiddos respond to our family dynamics, I came to recognize the impact of my own wiring on how I perceived my childhood. I am a super-sensitive, highly perceptive, and strong-willed soul. Another daughter in my family of origin might have just rolled with all the bumps in the road. I, however, rolled like a square log. *Thump. Thump. Thump.* Can you relate?

By God's grace, He put key people in my life to encourage me to get real about how I felt and to let go of the need to validate my pain. At one point I was able to sneak away for twenty-four hours to be alone with the Lord, and in that time I allowed every emotion to come to the surface. It wasn't pretty. As I sobbed over the unintentional hurts so fresh in my mind, I felt like they happened yesterday. As I prayed and read Scripture, it became crystal clear to me that God was more than able to handle my hurt and anger, and He was in a much better position than I to act as judge. Honesty before the Lord gave way to healing, and I was overwhelmed with compassion for my parents as I begged God for His mercy on them. I also asked forgiveness from God for my having harbored such bitterness and anger, when He so boldly tells us in the Word to forgive others as He has forgiven us (Matthew 6:14). Finally, I didn't need to hold on to anything from the past. I placed it in God's hands and felt a release to move forward.

Choosing to walk in forgiveness is a process—and in my case, has been years in the making—as I continually learn how to live in light of God's Word. Isn't it time you choose to walk in forgiveness too and experience the freedom God wants you to have?

How Do We Really Forgive?

When we choose to forgive an offense, we're saying, "I don't hold you in chains anymore, because I don't want you or this pain bound to me." Through your act of forgiveness, you hand over that person to God and trust Him to be the One who will judge every action fairly. As R. T. Kendall describes in *Total Forgiveness,*

> Reserving judgment for God alone shows that we are already beginning
> to forgive. We must leave to God how guilty our offenders are before
> Him.[28]

Forgiving others in the same way Christ forgave us unloads the weight of the wound onto the One who can carry it best.

Even if you can't imagine trusting God to handle the offenses that have marred your life, consider this fact: forgiveness not only sets you free from the one who hurt you, but it also enables God to forgive your offenses too. Oh yes, God made forgiveness a chain reaction:

> For if you forgive other people when they sin against you, your heavenly
> Father will also forgive you. But if you do not forgive others their sins, your
> Father will not forgive your sins. (Matthew 6:14–15)

Forgiveness also opens the door for reconciliation with a goal of restoration. But even when you can't or shouldn't pursue face-to-face reconciliation, it is still possible to trust God to work out the restoration process, as Kendall describes:

> Forgiveness and reconciliation are not always the same. Reconciliation
> requires the participation of two people.[29]

In the years following that season when I wholly forgave my parents, I experienced restoration in the relationship with my mom. We got our stuff out on the table, and God brought clarity to our misunderstandings and hurts. But the relationship with my dad actually turned in a devastating direction—my healing stirred up his hurts, and the pain led to more than four years of our not speaking to each other.

My heart was so grieved during those years, yet God used the rawness, hurt, and disappointment to draw me closer to Him. He grew my faith, challenging me to learn how to praise Him even if the story didn't end the way I wanted it to. The Lord eventually helped me totally forgive my father again, even though I had no contact with him. Oh, the peace that came over me after I surrendered the whole situation into His hands!

It took more than a year to walk out that process of forgiveness with the Lord before the feelings of hurt subsided. Then I could finally begin praying for my dad and asking God to bless him, even if we never saw each other again. You can imagine my shock the day I got an e-mail from my dad, filled with regret and asking for forgiveness as he owned his part in our mess. What a humbling but joyous moment it was when I was able to respond, "Yes, Dad. I've already forgiven you."

I've lost track of the number of years that have passed since that moment, but I can tell you this: God has restored the lost years, and our relationship feels all the more precious (Joel 2:25).

Forgiveness is an act you embrace in a moment, while the outcome is dependent on God's timing and tender intervention.

Cheryl and Jeff Scruggs share a moving story about forgiveness and reconciliation in their IAmSecond.com video. Cheryl describes how her behavior led to the demise of their marriage and, ultimately, to divorce. She owned her mistakes, confessing the pain she had brought upon her husband and family, as God convicted her about her behavior and her misplaced priorities. She yielded her life to the Lord and sought His forgiveness first, then went to her ex-husband. Her confession was pure. But there they stood in the aftermath. Forgiveness was on the table, but reconciliation was a long way off. As Jeff says, Cheryl needed to "make deposits in my trust account." It took more than seven years before that trust was rebuilt and redemption came into full bloom as they remarried.[30]

There is nothing like the freedom that comes from forgiving or being forgiven.

Yes, friend, His forgiveness is something you must embrace for yourself.

It's so easy to get stuck thinking you must be able to forgive yourself in order to move on, but really all you need to do is acknowledge your offenses before God and receive His forgiveness offered to you through His Son's death on the cross (Matthew 26:28). When Jesus paid the price for your sin, sister, your debt was reconciled once and for all. There is no need to carry it anymore. Will you lay it down before God today and move forward unchained? When you say yes to forgiveness, you're ultimately saying yes to living the life God intended.

Trap and Transform

The Walk of Forgiveness

God commands us to seek His forgiveness and to forgive others because it is good for us. It makes room for Him to dwell fully in our hearts. When we give Him permission to deal with our hurts and guilt and shame, He will bring about a radical transformation by changing us from the inside out.

Will you seek the Lord honestly in this matter of forgiveness? The questions and prompts below will guide you through the process, but before you begin, ask the Lord to open your spiritual eyes and bend your will to the Holy Spirit's leading. (Feel free to use initials and code words for the sake of privacy.)

Lord God, I seek You now about . . .

Help me see the offenses I have stored up in my heart that I need to give to You . . .

Help me acknowledge the part I've played in these situations and relationships . . .

Lord, please forgive me for . . .

Lord, please enable me to forgive these people . . .

Show me, Lord, where You were when these things happened to me . . .

God, please reveal to me truths from Your Word that I can cling to as I give You my hurts and choose to forgive . . .

Father, in this moment, I am choosing to forgive . . .

Lord, show me what steps I need to take toward reconciliation . . .

Go Deeper

1. If you gave God all the hurts stored up in your heart, how would your life be different?

2. What would it mean for you to walk through the process of biblical forgiveness? Describe what steps you'd take.

3. In light of all you've discovered about yourself and forgiveness, whom might God be calling you to share this information with?

Give It Over

Heavenly Father, show me what's going on in my heart so I can give it to You. Lead me in the process of forgiveness, and enable me to embrace Your healing work within my soul. Give me the courage and desire to forgive those who have hurt me. Change me from the inside out so that the fruit of my life will give You glory. In Jesus's name, amen. (Ephesians 4:31–32)

Phase 4

Stick with Solutions

What is God's will for my life?—is *not* the
right question. I think the right question is,
What is God's will? Once I know God's will,
then I can adjust my life to Him. In other
words, what is it that God is purposing
where I am? Once I know what God is doing,
then I know what I need to do. The focus
needs to be on *God*, not *my life*!

—HENRY BLACKABY

Your Starting Point

Growing in Your Relationship with God

In the morning, LORD, you hear my
voice; in the morning I lay my requests
before you and wait expectantly.

— PSALM 5:3

f you had to pick five "tools" that could help you become the new you, what would they be? Would you hire a house cleaner or personal trainer? (Ahem, both are on my bucket list!) Would you buy a new planner or download a task-list app for your smartphone? While these solutions may be worth the investment of your time and money, I have five key solutions that will leave a lasting impact on your life without putting a dent in your bank account.

I believe wholeheartedly that these solutions are essential in the process of change, because they build on a foundational attitude shift leading to healthier, new habits. Over the next week, we're going to look at each of these five solutions so you can put them into place in your life:

1. Cultivate an intimate relationship with God.
2. Live for an audience of one.
3. Build in margin.
4. Eliminate the excess and concentrate on the good.
5. Embrace mentoring relationships.

Friend, when these solutions become a part of who you are, your life will change radically! Ready to find out how?

What's Your Starting Point?

What's the first thing you do when you get out of bed? Do you check your e-mail on your phone or scroll through Facebook? Do you run to the coffeepot as you pray that the outfit you want to wear isn't still in the washing machine? (That is often my dilemma.) Or do you carefully plan out your morning with exercise and maybe even meeting with the Lord?

While my first bleary-eyed steps are toward some java, as soon as the kiddos head out the door for school, my focus shifts entirely as I nestle into my chair and grab my time with God. This is my starting point, which Christians often call quiet time or devotions. It's the time I set aside to read a chapter or two in my Bible and jot down some notes in my journal (because that's how I learn). I also spend time in prayer, usually journaling my thoughts and recording what God has to say to me. The format isn't as important as my heart's focus.

I need this time with God to get my mind and heart aligned with His perspective.

My starting point is sacred. It's like oxygen for my soul, but it hasn't always been this way. After becoming a Christian in college, I knew it was important to read my Bible but I didn't know where to start, nor did I feel compelled to figure it out. As I was coasting into my thirties, one of my best friends, Julie, and I were catching up over a long-overdue cup of coffee, as we tried to regain a sense of normal. Julie's husband was miraculously in remission after undergoing major treatment for a brain tumor over the course of the previous year. While I rambled on, complaining about the petty things happening in my life (compared to what Julie had been through), she sat there attentively and listened until she posed a question that made me squirm: "When are you going to get God off your to-do list and start having a real relationship with Him?"

Oh yeah! She nailed it. At that time in my life, my relationship with the Lord was not a priority. I was going through the motions of church and participating in a small group, but I wasn't spending any time with Him or reading the Scriptures. No wonder God felt distant.

I left that time with Julie convicted it was time to get real with God, but I didn't know how. The Lord, however, made it super simple. The next day, a friend from out of town showed up at my back door announcing that she felt led to give me a little devotional book by Ruth Myers called *The Satisfied Heart: 31 Days of Experiencing God's Love.* There was the answer: I decided that each afternoon I would read a chapter from the book and look up the suggested Bible verses. I dusted off a journal so that I could write out a verse and my prayers—something in me wanted evidence of this maturing step of faith.

More than ten years later, I'm in awe at the dozens of journals filled with prayers and packed in boxes tucked in the corner of my bedroom. I count it a miracle the way God moved me into desiring a deeper relationship with Him.

That one step of faith—that one spiritual discipline—was the starting point of living a changed life.

See, I couldn't come in contact with Scripture truth each day and not be impacted by it. Little by little, as I got to know God personally, my perspective on Him and my purpose in this world changed. My thinking was slowly transformed, and my attitudes and habits naturally followed suit. Initially I met with God during the girls' afternoon nap, but it eventually became a part of my morning routine. There is something beautiful about starting the day with the Lord and anticipating His unfolding work, as the psalmist describes:

In the morning, Lord, you hear my voice;
in the morning I lay my requests before you
and wait expectantly. (Psalm 5:3)

So, friend, what would you think about having a new starting point to your day? Would you let me kindly call you out too and urge you to get real with God by giving Him your time?

The Still Moment You Need

Honestly, friend, is it really that hard to find fifteen minutes in your day to sit quietly with the Lord and listen to His voice? He wants to speak to you, and He promises that you'll know it's Him. He is the Good Shepherd who calls His sheep:

After he has gathered his own flock, he walks ahead of them, and they
follow him because they know his voice. (John 10:4, NLT)

The Holy Spirit is at work in you, prompting you to follow His way (John
14:26). Guiding you in His truth! Speaking to your heart and mind.

The Mighty One, God, the LORD,
>   speaks and summons the earth
>   from the rising of the sun to where it sets. (Psalm 50:1)

Yes, God still speaks. Quietly. Purposefully. Truthfully.
So will you bend your heart to God and give Him everything inside? Will you
dig deep into the Word to find His voice? Will you turn your ear to Him, trusting
that He will speak to you? Will you make it your first priority to reach out to Him,
even before you contact a friend?

I call on you, my God, for you will answer me;
>   turn your ear to me and hear my prayer. (Psalm 17:6)

When you make this kind of quiet time the foundation on which you build
your life, you will see real life change happen. But remember, as Bible teacher Beth
Moore points out, it's a discipline that takes consistent cultivation and concerted
effort in the face of challenges and ever-changing emotions:

Sometimes physical exhaustion can make us feel spiritually dull, but that
passes with some rest. During dry times we trust the God-promised values
of prayer, worship, and Scripture reading, knowing they each bear fruit even
when we can't see it. God is ever-present no matter how sluggish our souls
feel toward Him.[31]

Yes, my friend, no matter how sluggish your soul might feel, you can't go wrong
in making your starting point time spent with the Lord. From Christ alone you will
draw your strength and find your focus to live your life with confidence. On John
Piper's blog we read,

Get alone with God and preach his word into your mind until your heart *sings* with confidence that you are new and cared for.[32]

I know it is hard to slow down and sit still before God, trusting Him with your time. Maybe that's why the command to "be still" is something we wrestle against, even though it opens the doorway to knowing God more fully (Psalm 46:10).

Being still with God is more than not moving . . . it's drawing closer to the Lord through getting to know Him in a whole new way.

It's experiencing His provisions and discovering His character as you dig into the Scriptures and see how He really functions. It's engaging with His Word so that you can learn what His voice sounds like and pay attention to how He says to live.

Trap and Transform

Cultivate Your Starting Point

Meeting with God daily doesn't have to be complicated, and with my Starting Point method, it couldn't be any simpler. In order to use the Starting Point method, you need to gather a few items:

- Pick a Bible or Bible app. If you'd like suggestions on how to find the right Bible, check out this overview: http://wp.me /p22Cdd-141.
- Pick a book in the Bible to study. I recommend starting with Psalms, one of the Gospels such as the book of John, or one of Paul's letters such as Ephesians. You can read the introductory notes to get a sense of what the book is about before you begin. If your Bible doesn't have introductory notes, go to BlueLetter Bible.org and look up the English Standard Version's "Introductions to the Books of the Bible": www.blueletterbible.org/study /intros/esv_intros.cfm.
- Grab a journal or notebook and a pen.
- Grab index cards for recording verses you'd like to memorize.

Once you have your supplies together, follow the routine outlined below to get into the Word by focusing on one chapter at a time.

- Every day read one chapter from Scripture.
- In your journal or on an index card, write down a verse or a promise that stands out to you, one you'd like to learn more about, then work toward memorizing it.
- Write down your prayers in a list form or as a letter to God. You might also want to try to turn a particular verse into a prayer.
- Sit still for a few minutes and ask God to speak to you. Jot down anything you feel you hear Him say and be sure to confirm it with Scripture. If you don't know how to do that, seek the input of a godly friend, mentor, or pastor.

Remember, the goal is consistency and quality, not quantity. It's a relationship with God you're building and a storehouse of the Word you're after. Be encouraged that when you sow this kind of effort, the fruit you will bear will be gloriously satisfying.

Go Deeper

1. Do you already have a habit of meeting with God daily? If so, what's worked in the past? If not, what keeps you from doing so?

2. When you study the Bible, do the words go in but never come out? How can you make it a richer and more fulfilling experience?

3. Could someone hold you accountable to embrace this Starting Point method? If so, what would that accountability relationship look like?

Give It Over

Lord God, thank You for wanting me to spend time with You! Please, Lord, give me the desire to store up Your Word in my heart and connect with You daily. Remove the obstacles in my way as I seek to start my days with You, listening for Your voice as I lay my burdens at the Cross. In Jesus's name, amen. (Psalm 17:6; 46:10)

Live for an Audience of One

The Art of Saying No

Am I now trying to win the approval of
human beings, or of God?

—GALATIANS 1:10

If I asked you whom or what are you living for, what would you say? I don't want the "good girl" answer. Give me the truth. Would you say, "I really want to live for God alone, but I know I'm too often worried by what others expect of me"? Are you like me, feeling as if you must answer to critics? Do you fear being rejected, even though you know that God has already chosen you? Maybe you're like the thousands of women who forget that they are "preapproved," as so cleverly worded by author Jennifer Dukes Lee in *Love Idol*.[33]

I see approval addiction time and time again with my life-coaching clients. The real issue is that it undermines a person's decision making and throws life out of balance, especially as people pleasers struggle with their inability to say no. Let's see if approval addiction is rearing its ugly head in your life and, if so, what solutions you can put in place to overcome it.

THE SIDE EFFECT OF APPROVAL ADDICTION

As a mother who has walked through the middle-school years with my oldest daughters, I can't help but wonder if this is the time in life when people pleasing, which is the beginning of approval addiction, takes root. Almost overnight, a beautiful, independent girl can crumble under the pressure to fit in. Was this your experience too? How did that time in life shape you?

Maybe peer influence didn't hit you as a ten-year-old but whopped you in high school or college. Was that when you began struggling to define your own values in the face of public opinion? Maybe today, as a grown woman, your need for approval defines your relationships with your parents or in-laws, friends or coworkers, fellow moms or even the church ladies. Oh yeah, even the church ladies!

One client was courageous enough to admit that she was stuck in her decision-making process because of the women in her church. These women had such strongly expressed opinions about how a young mom and wife should care for her family that my client was nearly paralyzed when making decisions about her life. She weighed every option in light of the potentially critical response she would have to face next time she attended Bible study or a Sunday morning service. So much for "What would Jesus do?" She was stuck with "What would the church ladies say?"

Their public opinion became personal, stamping her life with disapproval, when they should have encouraged her to seek the approval of the One who matters most.

The only way for her to break free of their influence was to recognize that their opinions were simply that. Their ideas weren't law or the Word of God being fitly applied. My client eventually realized that she needed to seek God for His opinion— being honest with Him in prayer, spending time studying Scripture, and seeking godly counsel from those who knew her and her situation well. The problem wasn't that the church ladies had uncharitable motives or gave unsound advice but rather that my client realized she had been wrong to live for their approval.

Can you see in your own life how easy it is to get caught up in living for the approval of well-meaning people?

How to Use a Pause, a Prayer, and a No

The struggle with approval addiction isn't just a modern-day problem, as Paul clearly calls attention to it:

Am I now trying to win the approval of human beings, or of God? Or am I trying to please people? If I were still trying to please people, I would not be a servant of Christ. (Galatians 1:10)

Paul spoke with such conviction about his own passion to please God that I believe it was a struggle for him to tune out the naysayers and critics. He mentioned this business of people pleasing more than once:

We are not trying to please people but God, who tests our hearts. (1 Thessalonians 2:4)

You and I know that the longing for approval and acceptance is real. Our desire to be approved causes us to make poor choices. Worse yet, instead of seeking God for His wisdom, we sometimes run from Him for fear that He might disapprove. Isn't it ironic that we sometimes fear man's disapproval more than God's?

Imagine what it would be like to seek God's approval above all else.

Friend, although I still struggle with seeking the approval of man, I can tell you that we can change our tendency and begin living for the approval of God. But to do so, we need some checks and balances:

1. *Pause.* Every time you have to make a decision, pause to reflect on your motives.
2. *Pray.* Before making a decision, talk with God about your motives, and seek His perspective on how to respond.
3. *Say no.* Say no to anything that taps into your approval-addiction tendencies and is not consistent with your God-given priorities—even if others don't understand.

Could it be that simple? Yes and no. Turning to God with every decision will require discipline and commitment. That will be the hard part! But once you establish the habit, you will find it easier to stay focused on heeding God's leading rather than pursuing your own or others' desires.

Ongoing, never-ending, always-open communication with God combats approval addiction like nothing else.

Pausing to check your motives and turning to God in prayer is more than a five-minute game delay—it's an opportunity for God to speak to you, especially on any decision that might lead to a change in your responsibilities, relationships, and resources. As long as analysis paralysis doesn't set in, it's okay to pause and pray, even for days, weeks, or months before making a decision. If your desire is to live for God alone, then taking this time to consult Him on your decisions is totally worthwhile.

Oh, I know—some of us just don't want to wait on a decision. But waiting, praying, and communicating with God will change a life driven by approval addiction into one that is guided by God's purposes.

So, why don't we find out how to take that powerful pause in order to make *no* a part of your "new you" vocabulary and to say *yes* to God's leading more purposefully?

Trap and Transform

The Art of Saying No

Do you have a habit of thinking and praying before saying yes? Would you say you're pretty good at using the word *no,* or is it a struggle to put those two little letters together? Learning how to say no is a skill you can develop as you seek to understand your motives and have go-to scripts ready to use when the need arises.

Step 1: Face the Facts and Consider Priorities

Read through the following "Should I say yes or no?" evaluation questions. Consider how you could use them in the face of your next decision as you seek to focus on God's approval. You might want to rewrite these questions on an index card and keep them by your desk or in your Bible.

1. What is being asked of me? (Be specific in terms of time, date, resources, finances.)
2. How will it impact my other responsibilities?
3. Do I have the skill set to fulfill this responsibility or opportunity?
4. Is this something I've always wanted to do, or is this something I feel I ought to do because of what others expect of me?

5. Is this something that I can say no to now but yes to at a better time in my life?
6. Is this something that feels straight from the hand of God? If so, has this been confirmed by others who have no vested interest?
7. What will it cost my loved ones?
8. Do my loved ones, especially my fellow Christians, support this decision?
9. What is my motive for saying yes to this opportunity? Whose approval am I ultimately seeking?
10. What will I have to say no to if I say yes to this?

Step 2: Preparing Your Pause-and-Pray Script

Learning how to say no to others takes practice. Consider how these pause-and-pray scripts can keep you from saying yes without first consulting God:

- "Thank you for asking me to do _____. I have a policy of not saying yes to any opportunity without spending time in prayer and talking with my family/spouse. I'll get back to you by _____."
- "Thank you for asking me. It sounds exciting. I'll get back to you by _____."

Write out your script so that you can take time to pause, pray, and make a wise decision.

If you decide to say no, consider how you could use one of these grace-filled responses:

- "I'm so glad you took the time to consider me for _____. Thank you for giving me time to pray and think about it. As I've evaluated what's on my plate, I can see it would be unwise to say yes at this time."

- "I was honored by your invitation; however, after I've evaluated my time and talked with _____, I realize I can't make the commitment to you at this time. If the opportunity arises in the future, please feel free to contact me."
- "I'm so glad you asked me to do _____. As I've considered this opportunity, I've realized that as much as I want to say yes, it is really not the best timing [or a good fit]. Would you let me start _____ instead? Or could I do _____ for you instead?"

What other "just say no" scripts could you have ready to use?

Go Deeper

1. Does your need for approval make it impossible to say no to opportunities? Describe why or why not.

2. When have you said yes when you should have said no? What did you learn from that experience?

3. What situations do you need to say no to today? How can you make healthy changes in that direction?

Give It Over

Heavenly Father, You know the motives of my heart. You see when I make commitments because I want to do Your work and honor You, and when I'm just interested in pleasing others. Please help me grow in the art of saying no. Help me fight this desire for approval and remind me that You already approve of me. In Jesus's name, amen. (Galatians 1:10; 1 Thessalonians 2:4)

Make Room for Margin

Cut Back and Carve Out

> He cuts off every branch in me that
> bears no fruit, while every branch that
> does bear fruit he prunes so that it will
> be even more fruitful.
>
> —John 15:2

Do you think you have margin in your life? In other words, do you have space in your schedule to respond to the unexpected without a meltdown? Do you have regularly scheduled rest and relaxation and nonworking vacations? My guess is that spare time may not be a part of your routine because the norm is to have a "marginless" life, as Dr. Richard A. Swenson describes:

> Marginless is the disease of the new millennium. . . .
>
> The marginless lifestyle is a relatively new invention and one of progress's most unreasonable ideas. Yet in a very short time it has become a nearly universal malady. Few are immune. It is not limited to a certain socioeconomic group, nor a certain educational level. Even those with a deep spiritual faith are not spared. Its pain is impartial and nonsectarian—everybody gets to have some.[34]

Maybe your marginless life is dictated by a never-ending to-do list. Maybe you struggle with knowing how to keep your responsibilities within reasonable limits.

Maybe you feel you do a pretty good job at balancing your schedule, then suddenly something goes wrong. *Whammo!* You're out of your routine and totally overwhelmed.

Friend, it may be time to cut back and carve out in order to make room for margin. Let's look at how to build margin into your new routine while also seeking God to determine what needs to be pruned to make space in your life to breathe and grow.

THE EPIDEMIC OF MARGINLESSNESS

A marginless life has no white space. It's jam-packed with commitments and obligations, chores and projects, relationships and responsibilities. It doesn't leave room for watching a movie on Friday night or reading a book on Saturday afternoon. It doesn't allow for an afternoon off to spend time with a hurting friend or taking a tech-free, out-of-the-office vacation. It doesn't even leave room to get out of the house without running late to every appointment.

A marginless life not only costs in missed opportunities; like an abrasive irritant, it rubs life raw.

Think about how you feel when you run out of time. Are you cranky, critical, and downright miserable? The kiddo gets sick, and you nearly implode because you just don't have time for it. Or you're on vacation but panicked because you remember you forgot to reply to that one person who had been waiting on you since last week. Or maybe you can't find your car keys, and so now you're twenty minutes late to that doctor's appointment—because you always run ten minutes late. Ahem. I've been guilty of that! How about you?

A marginless life doesn't leave room for the unexpected.

And life is full of surprises and mishaps, which means we will fall behind, forget that one thing, and find ourselves failing on a normal day. If you and I don't build margin into our schedules, we'll be chronically late, unprepared, overwhelmed, frustrated, and worn down.

In contrast, can you imagine, however, what a life with margin might feel like? What if you were on time, prepared, and rested? How would that change the way you feel about yourself? What if you could take a day off or even a week away without guilt? What if you were able to leave that project hanging in the balance while responding to a friend in need? Wouldn't that feel awesome?

Friend, it's possible to create a life with margin, but it requires cutting back on commitments and carving out unscheduled time.

It might mean turning down a ministry position for the sake of managing the rest of your life with better balance. Maybe it looks like each family member cutting back on one extracurricular activity simply to save the runaround time.

If you want margin in your life, you're going to have to buck what you think is expected or required so you can create a life that works. Does that sound scary or liberating? I hope the latter, especially as you seek the Lord to understand what He wants your life to look like.

When God Prunes

One fall morning, I was deadheading old blooms in our rose garden when God gave me a visual about the beauty of pruning. I had been talking with Him about feeling overcommitted but not knowing what needed to change. I told Him I felt I was *underparticipating* in this life He'd given me. There was simply not enough time to accomplish everything, and at the end of the day my disappointment oozed all over everyone. So I begged the Lord to show me the way out of this cycle. What did God have to say in response? He reminded me about how things grow:

> *Your life is like this rose garden. There are a lot of bushes here. There's potential for a beautiful season of blooms. But pruning needs to happen in order for growth to occur. Without pruning, this garden will be full of pathetic-looking, bloomless bushes.*
>
> *So will you let Me prune you? Will you let Me prune not only your schedule but also pull the weeds from your heart? Will you lay down the things you think you must do and let Me reprioritize your life?*

I could suddenly see how all those rosebushes represented my responsibilities and relationships, and that the roses would never bloom if I didn't cut back. I needed to better invest in the most important relationships and responsibilities. It was time for God-sized pruning.

> He cuts off every branch in me that bears no fruit, while every branch that
> does bear fruit he prunes so that it will be even more fruitful. (John 15:2)

I faced the cutback because I longed to see the fruit.

As I looked at my life map and time-evaluation worksheet (oh yes, I've used these long before becoming a life coach), I saw that my priorities were out of whack and the only solution was to step back from certain commitments. While I was busy doing good things, they weren't the best things for my life in that season. I was simply overcommitted, and as a result I was neglecting my family and home and my time with the Lord. As I prayed about how to resolve this imbalance, I knew the Lord was asking me to lay down my blogging, writing, and speaking. I also knew it was time to walk away from leading a mentoring group for teens. It was as though He was stripping me down to the basics. While it generated a raw, uncomfortable feeling, His pruning actually freed me up to rebuild my life according to the priorities I sensed He wanted me to live with from that point forward.

As painful as it is to experience a God pruning, it's worth the fruit.

At first, I didn't know what to do with my new free time. I was so used to being overbooked that having margin in each day felt strange and intimidating. Yet as the weeks unfolded, God showed me ways to heal in this sabbatical-like season. I began spending more time with Him, and my faith grew immensely because I was steeped in the Word and prayer. I also met one on one with a friend who fed my faith and emphasized the importance of fellowship. Seeing the fruit of being available to my family, especially in the evenings, also changed my entire perspective on when I should work in the future.

As I emerged from that season of pruning, I was indeed a new woman in terms of how I decided to use my time.

I created a work-free zone after five o'clock every evening.

I made time to connect with friends each week.

I stopped doing ministry alone and partnered with others.

I stayed off the computer on Friday and Saturday nights so I could watch movies with my family.

I planned ahead for work-free vacations.

As I look back on that season, I thank God for it. He really did rebuild my routine and priorities through creating margin in my life, and the fruit that has come from that season has radically blessed my family and laid a foundation for the life I'm leading now—a life I love!

By God's grace, I surrendered to His pruning.

Is it time for you to surrender to His pruning too?

Trap and Transform

Cut Back and Carve Out

Are you ready to build a fresh new schedule with ample margin? You'll have to start using that "just say no" script from Day 17 more often in order to say yes to the opportunities God brings your way. You'll also have to consider your God-given wiring and clearly defined priorities to determine how to focus on your responsibilities, relationships, and resources. Yes, everything you've been learning on this journey is finally coming together as you determine what your new life is supposed to look like!

Planning for margin will lay the foundation for the life God intends you to lead.

The steps below will take you through the process, but remember to enter into it with prayer, asking God for His wisdom and direction.

Step 1: What Does Your Real Schedule Look Like?

Grab your time-evaluation worksheet and life map (from Days 1 and 2) to help you answer these questions:

1. What have you left out of your normal routine that you need to include going forward?

2. What do you need to eliminate from your routine?

3. As you consider your new, ideal schedule, what high-priority respon-sibilities or relationships do you need to schedule first?

Step 2: Create a New Schedule with Margin

Grab a clean copy of the time-evaluation worksheet and use it to create your schedule with margin. Have a calendar on hand, as you'll be blocking off sea-sonal margin time too.

1. *Blocked-Off Margin.* For every commitment, schedule time on either side of it. This way you are setting aside time for things like getting out of the house and returning home, along with a few minutes to deal with the unexpected, like lost keys, kids who can't find shoes, and the UPS guy who shows up as you are pulling out.

2. *Daily Margin.* This time should come in blocks of a half hour or more each day to leave room for the unexpected God appointments, such as receiving a phone call from a friend or caring for the needs of a sick child, as well as the usual last-minute errands or a project that takes longer than expected. If every second is booked, then the unexpected leads to stress and falling behind.

3. *Weekly Margin.* This time should be a few hours a week, grouped together on at least two to three different days, to allow you to rest or catch up on life. Maybe you'll use your weekly margin to read a book, take a nap, go on a walk, or watch a movie. Maybe you'll choose to use this time to clean the pileup on the kitchen counter or make a phone call to a friend. Remember, weekly margin time shouldn't be used to get ahead, as that would defeat

the purpose of putting a stop to the crazy cycle. The goal is to use weekly margin as a time to breathe. If you keep stealing from it, then you need to cut back on responsibilities until this sacred time stays untouched.

4. *Seasonal Margin.* Block out seasonal margin on your calendar so you can pull back from your normal rhythms for at least two days or more. It's a sabbath for the mind, body, and soul. Maybe it comes in the form of a family vacation or weekend getaway. It may be a stay-cation experience, a time when you take in the local sights and put the everyday chores of life on hold.

Go through this process again every three months (as your commitments will inevitably change) or whenever you go through a major life change.

Go Deeper

1. Before now, has your life had margin space built in? How is that working for you? What would you like to change?

2. What do you think God wants to prune in your life so you may experience growth?

3. As you consider the process of cutting back, knowing that it might be painful, what can motivate you to continue to embrace this process? In other words, what do you think might be the rewards ahead?

✳ Give It Over

Heavenly Father, I invite You to prune my life. I want to fulfill Your purposes and priorities, not my agendas and foolish doings. Show me, Lord, how to carve out margin so that I can enjoy the life You've given me and be able to respond to the special needs or demands You unexpectedly send my way. In Jesus's name, amen. (John 15:2)

The Beauty of Less

*Eliminate the Excess and
Concentrate on What's Best*

> For where your treasure is,
> there your heart will be also.
>
> —MATTHEW 6:21

Now that you have a concept of margin when it comes to your schedule, how about considering what it would look like to have space within your home and maybe even office? Yes, I know that whole books have been devoted to simple living, decluttering, and organizing, so even to approach this topic may seem crazy, but I think it's worth it! Why? Because that stuff piled up in your home may very well be stealing your time, slowing you down, and keeping you from living life the way God intended.

Let me confess, I like my stuff. I like my mementos. I like my accessories. Even so, I've discovered the truth in what my mother always says: "The more stuff you have, the more time you have to devote to caring for it." I also believe that the more stuff you have, the more distractions you'll be faced with daily. When it comes to distractions, I'd like to keep them to a minimum. I want to live this life to the fullest but not be bogged down with things, kind of like one of my favorite bloggers and the founder of the Art of Simple, Tsh Oxenreider.[35] This woman is inspiring with her adventurous, not-trapped-by-stuff lifestyle, and she spurs me on to live unhindered in my own way.

We don't have to become like Tsh or the newest guru of simple living—let's leave that to the experts. But I'd love to see you launch your new self emboldened by the ability to live an uncluttered life that frees you to explore your passions and purposes without any unnecessary junk in your proverbial trunk.

The Liberating Art of Eliminating and Concentrating

Imagine getting rid of all your piles, crammed-up closets, and jam-packed storage units so you can live free from the weight of them. Imagine if you finally let it *all* go in the pursuit of living with less and trusting God even more.

Eliminating and concentrating will enable you to focus on the good things, great relationships, and life-giving opportunities God brings into your life.

That's what I witnessed happening for one of my life-coaching clients. Evelyn wanted to create space in her home for guests, especially for her niece to stay with her during school breaks. But she lived in a small apartment with a tiny second room that served as her office, storage space, and guest room. All the papers, books, and keepsakes created wall-to-wall obstacles, not only in terms of a guest even getting to the bed, but in Evelyn's feeling as if she couldn't be hospitable when a need arose.

So, Evelyn and I worked to conquer the clutter. She made a plan for how to tackle each area of the guest room, determining what she needed to eliminate (trash, recycle, or repurpose) and what she needed to concentrate on (carefully selecting keepers based on purpose and assigning each one a spot). After devoting a few hours a week toward the task, she finally made headway and invited friends to visit. The delight of having guests over was a great incentive to keep up the habit and gave Evelyn the motivation to conquer other areas of her home. Her takeaway was this:

I don't want my stuff to keep me from living this life I've been given.

Eliminating and concentrating means evaluating the purpose of your stuff and its value in light of eternity. Oh no, God isn't focused on giving us stuff, because He knows that it will amount to nothing in the end:

Do not store up for yourselves treasures on earth, where moths and vermin destroy, and where thieves break in and steal. But store up for yourselves treasures in heaven, where moths and vermin do not destroy, and where thieves do not break in and steal. For where your treasure is, there your heart will be also. (Matthew 6:19–21)

If your stuff has no eternal purpose and it's robbing your emotional reserves, isn't it time to eliminate all that from your life and concentrate on joining God in His eternal work? Anne Ortlund describes it this way:

You have noticed my using the words "eliminate and concentrate." I think they're two words that are key to good living.

You want to manage your time? You eliminate and concentrate on your goals. You want to disciple? You eliminate crowds and concentrate on a few people.

You want to keep a sharp wardrobe, before the Lord Jesus? Eliminate the unnecessary, concentrate on a few "right" outfits in one color scheme.[36]

Anne is onto something here, don't you think? She lays out a pattern for discerning how to use your time and minimize distractions. Eliminating and concentrating doesn't just create a decluttered and organized home; it also helps us carefully and intentionally cut out whatever is unnecessarily consuming time and depleting finances. Yes, even money comes under the fine-tuning of eliminating and concentrating. Just think of what would happen if you spent less time and money on stuff and more investing in the lives of the people God has put in your life and on your heart. I love the way financial guru Dave Ramsey puts this in perspective:

No amount of stuff will ever give you contentment or fulfillment. If I buy a new ski boat, I do it because I know my family and I want it and will enjoy it, not because *that thing* will make me happy. It won't. Money can buy fun, but it can't buy happiness.[37]

Eliminating and concentrating lets you live unhindered by pressure to have more so that you can actually enjoy the life God's given you.

Some of our stuff serves only as a functional god—yes, idolatry once again—as you and I get trapped into believing that these possessions will meet a need only

God can fill. That, my friend, is the heart of the issue, and why it's worth considering what we need to get rid of and what we need to focus on.

Think about all that you have crammed into every nook and cranny of your life. Roam through your closets. Peek into your cabinets. Brave the storage room. How much of it did you purchase to pacify an emotional hurt? What are you holding on to simply because a loved one gave it to you, even though you don't need it or like it? How much of your stuff serves as an ineffective security blanket?

It's a Process That Forms a Habit

Eliminating and concentrating is a mind-set shift. You give up the habit of needing it all and needing it now, while deciding what to allow into your life and keep around for the long haul. As you approach this new habit, two questions can help you make wise choices:

1. Should I eliminate _____ from my life because it is keeping me from . . .
   - living according to my God-given priorities and purposes?
   - pursuing life-changing relationships?
   - embracing God-given opportunities?
   - being wise with the use of my resources?
2. Should I choose to concentrate on _____ so that I can . . .
   - use my time for God-given priorities and purpose?
   - guard my emotional reserves for the sake of serving and engaging with others?
   - care for my health and continue to join God in His work?
   - use my money more wisely with a goal of saving and giving?

These aren't arbitrary decisions. They are based on scriptural principles as you consider how your stuff can become a hang-up rather than a blessing, blocking you from joining God in the work He has for you each day. As we always said to our toddlers, "People are more important than things." And yet, we love our things, right? So how about we make sure that we love in the right order: God first, people second, and everything else third.

Friend, embracing the beauty of less and making room in your life to more fully engage with the people and opportunities God places before you will set the stage for the life you really do want to live.

Trap and Transform

Eliminate-and-Concentrate Challenge

Learning how to eliminate and concentrate is a process that will take time and practice. Use the steps below to make a plan for the areas you want to focus on first. Pace yourself so that you can experience success by accomplishing one task at a time. It's easy to get excited about the potential outcome and bite off more than you can chew, so be reasonable in terms of what you want to tackle first, then schedule time for focusing on each goal.

Step 1: Deciding What to Eliminate and Where to Concentrate

Looking at the list below, which stuff do you need to focus on eliminating, and where do you need to concentrate your attention? Check off all that apply.

❏ Books and CDs
❏ Clothing
❏ Commitments
❏ Décor
❏ Garage and tools
❏ Gifts
❏ Habits
❏ Hobbies
❏ Kitchen items
❏ Memorabilia
❏ Sports equipment
❏ Technology
❏ Technology usage
❏ Other: _____

As you think about this process, prayerfully consider whether you might have some measure of emotional attachment to these particular items. You may need to address that attachment through the help of a professional Christian counselor in order to let go of your stuff. Don't be shy about asking for help. Sometimes a conversation is all it takes to bring about that "aha" moment and be set free.

Step 2: Set Some Goals and Get Organized

As you look at the list above, pick three areas that you want to focus on over the next three months. Make a list of all your stuff as it pertains to those areas, and use the following categories to decide what to do with it. When the time comes to actually work on that project, use these categories in your sorting:

T—Trash
R—Recycle or Repurpose
D—Donate
F—Find a Home for the Item Within Your Space
S—Seasonal Storage

First Focus (Month 1):

Second Focus (Month 2):

Third Focus (Month 3):

Step 3: Going Forward

One way to stay on top of the areas in which you've eliminated and concentrated is to create mini-preference guides that enable you to make wise choices in the future. It's especially easy to do this when it comes to your clothing and household décor. For example, you might create something like a "capsule wardrobe" (using a guide like this one: www.elisapulliam.com/2014/09/10/creating-capsule-wardrobe) to help define the type of clothing you like and focus your purchases in the future. Take a few minutes to brainstorm what types of preference guides might be helpful for you and how you'd go about making them.

Go Deeper

1. Is the stuff in your life a metaphor for something deeper going on in your soul? In other words, are you hanging on to things for comfort and security when God is calling you to trust Him more?

2. As you think of the principle of eliminating and concentrating, what do you find most exciting about the process? How do you want to implement this in your life?

3. What's most intimidating about eliminating and concentrating? Who can come alongside and support you in this process?

Give It Over

Heavenly Father, thank You for Your reminder that what I have on earth can't go with me to heaven and that whatever I hold on to has the power to rule my life. Please, Lord, teach me the art of eliminating and concentrating so that I may focus on storing up my treasures in heaven alone. In Jesus's name, amen. (Matthew 6:19–21)

Don't Go It Alone

*Cultivate Mentoring Relationships
Through Listening Well*

Teach the older women. . . . These older
women must train the younger women.

—Titus 2:3–4, nlt

As we round the bend to the last straightaway, we have one last solution to embrace: how to cultivate mentoring relationships. Friend, you're not meant to go through this journey alone. You need to be in mentoring relationships with other women, both those older and younger than you. Why?

Because you have much to learn from the generation that has gone before you and just as much to pour into the one that is following close on your heels.

This interconnectedness can serve as a life-support system, if you'll admit that you need others in the first place. That might mean you'll have to quit "tivving," as we say in my family. Let me explain. We've come to use the word *tivving* to gently remind one another not to let stubborn pride take over. We coined this term after watching a Discovery Channel documentary about storm chasers and found ourselves in awe at the way a Tornado Intercept Vehicle (TIV) functions.

A TIV is designed to drive into the eye of a storm to record scientific data. When a TIV is parked, its suspension allows it to become flush to the ground, then spikes are driven into the dirt to anchor it against the tornado-force winds. A TIV isn't going anywhere when it's locked down. Thus, for our family, *tivving* describes a person who is refusing to budge from his or her position—it's the worst form of stubbornness, usually laced with insecurity, pride, a bit of idolatry, and excuses of every kind.

So what do tivving and mentoring have to do with each other? Most women get quite tivvy when it comes to mentoring. Insecurity, fear, and pride kick into overdrive, and instead of doing life side by side with transparency and humility, they isolate themselves and put on masks to cover up their shortcomings. Hmm. Does that sound like something you're prone to do? I know I've struggled with this. But this is not how God wants us to live, friend.

In fact, guarding ourselves against transparent mentoring relationships costs us the opportunity to grow spiritually and emotionally under the influence of some truly amazing women. As you launch on the journey of transformation, I challenge you to seek out a mentor who can cheer you on, while you bravely invite a younger gal along on the journey too.

Because We Need One Another

God has called us to be in community with others, especially as one generation of women to another. Some call this *discipleship,* where the focus is on studying the Bible together and drawing out real-life applications. I take this idea of discipleship a bit further and call it *biblical mentoring,* in which the teaching takes places in the classroom of life.

Biblical mentoring happens when the older generation comes alongside the younger one, encouraging and equipping with relevant, Scripture-based truth as it pertains to everyday life.

Mentoring isn't dictated by age, experience, or a sense of qualification. It can happen between a mother and her teenage daughter, between a thirty-something momma coming alongside a twenty-something college gal, an aunt coming alongside a tween-age niece, or an elderly neighbor coming alongside an empty nester.

Biblical mentoring can take place while cooking dinner together or packing up a house for a major move. It can happen in a ministry context, such as planning a women's conference or teaching Sunday school. It may occur while sharing a cup of coffee or doing a Bible study together. It can be formal, as in meeting once a month, or informal, simply by serving together in a particular task.

Think about how you may have been mentored in the past without even know-ing it. Yes, it could be that simple and that informal!

Biblical mentoring means following Christ purposefully while inviting the next generation to join the journey.

This is exactly what Paul described:

> Similarly, teach the older women to live in a way that honors God. They
> must not slander others or be heavy drinkers. Instead, they should teach
> others what is good. These older women must train the younger women
> to love their husbands and their children, to live wisely and be pure, to work
> in their homes, to do good, and to be submissive to their husbands. Then
> they will not bring shame on the word of God. (Titus 2:3–5, NLT)

I've always found it intriguing that Paul describes in detail what the older women ought to do to train the younger women, and how those challenges are still plaguing us today. Instructing women to care for their families and homes and to train the next generation is a high calling that is not without sacrifice. We need one another because it's too hard to go it alone—and it's not necessary to learn the ropes by trial and error.

Additionally, the way we care for our families and homes has tremendous im-pact not only on our loved ones but also on those looking on—our actions have the power to make the gospel attractive, or do the opposite. That's why it's beneficial to learn from the older generation. It's about our legacy as well as our impact on the kingdom of God.

Biblical mentoring is part of a bigger mission: sharing the good news of Jesus Christ as we serve those in our midst and become witnesses to those watching how we live.

What would it take for you to engage in heart-deep, life-changing, biblical-mentoring relationships?

Listening Well Makes the Difference

Listening well sets the stage for healthy mentoring relationships because it changes the purpose from *teaching* and *telling* to *encouraging* and *equipping.* People often misunderstand mentoring: we *don't* have to know the answers to everyone's problems. Nor do we have to tell someone what to do, even though that is our default tendency. Rather, a better approach is for us to use questions to help people figure out the right next steps for themselves.

The problem with telling someone what to do is that the person receiving the instruction doesn't own the solution.

A better way to go about mentoring is to learn how to listen well and ask questions to enable a mentoree to solve her own problems. Then she will own the solution . . . and you'll be less frustrated too. This approach also removes the pressure to have all the answers and leads to healthy, life-giving relationships. This is exactly what transpired between Moses and his father-in-law, Jethro (Exodus 18).

Let me set the stage: Moses was leading the Israelites to the Promised Land when Jethro came for a visit. Upon their meeting, Moses recounted all that God had done in rescuing the people from Pharaoh and slavery in Egypt, telling Jethro about the hardships they experienced and how the Lord saved them. Jethro's response is priceless, not only because he made time to listen to his son-in-law, but also because he was "delighted to hear about all the good things" and praised the Lord with Moses (Exodus 18:7–9). Jethro affirmed Moses and built up their relationship while laying a foundation for speaking wisdom into his life. While Jethro had something to *tell* Moses, he did so only after listening to him—and then he approached with questions:

> The next day Moses took his seat to serve as judge for the people, and they stood around him from morning till evening. When his father-in-law saw all that Moses was doing for the people, he said, "What is this you are doing for the people? Why do you alone sit as judge, while all these people stand around you from morning till evening?"
>
> Moses answered him, "Because the people come to me to seek God's will. Whenever they have a dispute, it is brought to me, and I decide between the parties and inform them of God's decrees and instructions." (verses 13–16)

Jethro didn't barge in with instructions. He didn't take over and do it himself. He gave Moses a chance to explain himself and then offered wisdom:

Moses' father-in-law replied, "What you are doing is not good. You and these people who come to you will only wear yourselves out. The work is too heavy for you; you cannot handle it alone. Listen now to me and I will give you some advice, and may God be with you. . . . If you do this and God so commands, you will be able to stand the strain, and all these people will go home satisfied." (verses 17–19, 23)

Isn't it amazing how much easier it is to receive advice if you first feel you've been heard, trusted, affirmed, and supported? Maybe that's why it was so natural for Moses to respond accordingly:

Moses listened to his father-in-law and did everything he said. (verse 24)

I believe Jethro's words mattered to Moses not only because he was family but also because of the winsome way Jethro approached Moses—first by listening to him and then by approaching with wise questions. That, my friend, is the art of listening well and cultivating a life-changing, mentoring relationship. Imagine what it would feel like to have a Jethro in your life or become that type of person to someone else.

Trap and Transform

Make Mentoring and Listening Part of Your Life

Are you ready to brainstorm ways to make mentoring part of your life and to learn how to listen well? I hope so, as having even one or two meaningful connections with older and younger women will make this journey of transformation that much more rewarding. Remember this truth, my friend: *While you're still in progress and becoming the woman God intended, you can be of great influence on the next generation.*

The questions below will provide you a way to prayerfully talk with God about finding a mentor for yourself and stepping into the role of mentor for someone else. Following those questions, you'll find a little guide on how to begin to listen well in all your relationships.

Step 1: Embrace Mentoring

1. What excuses stand in the way of finding a mentor or being a mentor? How can you trump this tivviness with the truth?

2. Whom do you think God might be calling you to mentor? What steps can you take to reach out to this person?

3. Are there one or two people that you would like as your mentors? Jot down ideas about what you'd like to learn from them.

4. What steps can you take toward engaging with those older women, such as inviting them for coffee or making a call?

Step 2: Learn to Listen Well

There are six key aspects of listening well. As you look at this list, circle the top two that you'd like to focus on over the next few weeks, then begin practicing those skills in all your conversations.

1. *Engage your body.* Engage in a conversation not only with speech but also with your posture and body language by making eye contact, nodding your head, and focusing on the other person.

2. *Embrace the silence.* Slow down your speaking and mental multitasking in order for you to focus on the other person.

3. *Ask questions prayerfully.* Prayerfully ask God what questions to ask rather than focusing on what you want to share.

4. *Avoid the why question.* Open with "Would you" or "How can you" instead of "Why did you" questions to avoid making the person feel defensive.

5. *Restate and affirm.* Listen in such a way that you can restate and affirm what you hear by repeating the person's last sentence or summarizing what you heard her say.

6. *Skip the lecture and story.* Refrain from lecturing in order to focus on asking questions. Resist the urge to tell a personal story. If you feel you have one that is relevant, ask permission to share it and keep it super short.

Go Deeper

1. Is tivving keeping you from experiencing healthy mentoring relationships? How?

2. How can focusing on intentional, biblical mentoring transform the way you look at the relationships in your life?

3. What keys to listening more effectively do you want to practice today?

ꙅive It Over

Heavenly Father, thank You for designing me not to go through life alone. God, reveal to me the older women with whom I naturally connect and how I can learn from them by listening to their wisdom. Lord, also show me how to engage women of the next generation by inviting them to do life with me. In Jesus's name, amen. (Titus 2:3–5)

Phase 5

A Vibrant New Vision

What you do today is shaped by what
you believe about tomorrow.

—TIMOTHY KELLER

Embrace the New You

Define Your Vision and Set Your Goals

> Not that I have already obtained all this,
> or have already arrived at my goal, but I
> press on to take hold of that for which
> Christ Jesus took hold of me.
>
> —Philippians 3:12

I t's amazing how much the transformation process is like watching children grow up. You may hardly notice how their bodies are developing, minds are expanding, and hearts are exploding from one day to the next. Well, unless you know someone like my middle daughter, who grew almost three inches in three months right before she turned thirteen. In her case, we could tell transformation was underway simply by seeing her pants becoming capris. But for most of us, authentic life transformation isn't that obvious, nor does it happen that quickly.

Real transformation doesn't happen overnight—it takes a series of overnights to see the impact of each attitude shift leading to a focused habit change.

With each intentional step toward whole life change, a new woman emerges. Friend, since you've made it this far through the journey, I am sure that is where you are today. You are in the beginning stages of meeting the new woman you desire to become, while anticipating what the Lord is going to accomplish in and through you in the days ahead. Even though this leg of the race is coming to a close, it's time to put on your spiritual running shoes and press on to the finish line.

Not that I have already obtained all this, or have already arrived at my goal, but I press on to take hold of that for which Christ Jesus took hold of me. (Philippians 3:12)

Do you see your goal, my friend, tucked into that verse? Imagine the prize of seeing Jesus face to face, knowing that you gave Him your all in this lifetime! Imagine the delight of knowing you yielded to His ways, embraced His purposes, and joined Him in His work. Oh, the reward that will be: finally to see Him and know that you lived every last breath for Him. May that vision motivate you to walk . . . or maybe even run . . . boldly forward, embracing the truth so that the Lord may set you free to become the woman He intended.

Ready, Set, Vision

Before you close this book, I want you to have a plan in place to help you hold to your mission of becoming the new you—a woman who is "brighter and more beautiful" as she follows Jesus every passing day (2 Corinthians 3:18, MSG). That plan requires a vision statement along with clear, measurable goals, so that from time to time you can meet with the Lord and reflect on where you are, what still needs to change, and where you want to head in the short and long term.

Casting vision doesn't mean you boss God around or set forth pie-in-the-sky dreams. Instead the goal is to pursue practical, concrete steps while making yourself accountable to God through time spent praying about your future, all the while knowing that the Lord ultimately determines your steps.

In their hearts humans plan their course,
   but the LORD establishes their steps. (Proverbs 16:9)

You and I can come up with great plans—the Lord gives us permission to do so! But the beauty of being a child of God is that His plans trump ours. He'll determine our steps, and for that we can be quite grateful. So what's the point of planning? Planning and casting vision actually becomes a way to grow our faith because we see God's miraculous reroutings and unexpected blessings. So how about taking a step in faith, putting some vision and goals on paper, and making a plan to connect with God about them in a few months? I'm certain your investment of time will be well worth it!

Casting Your Vision

As you think about this journey and the direction you sense God taking you, I want to encourage you to find your inspiration in Scripture. Take time to search for a Bible verse that captures the way you feel God is working in you and calling you to live. For example, one verse that has shaped my life focus for more than a decade comes from Ephesians:

> I became a servant of this gospel by the gift of God's grace given me through the working of his power. (3:7)

That verse settled in me when I understood that my life was truly a gift of His grace and His power clearly, abundantly working in me. But it's not the only verse that's marked my life. The truth that I am chosen by God has been critical to understanding my identity and life purpose in Christ more recently, especially as I reflect often on these verses:

> But you are a chosen people, a royal priesthood, a holy nation, God's special possession, that you may declare the praises of him who called you out of darkness into his wonderful light. (1 Peter 2:9)

> You did not choose me, but I chose you and appointed you so that you might go and bear fruit—fruit that will last. (John 15:16)

My vision statement is continually growing in depth and breadth as I mature in my faith and experience twists and turns in life. As you seek to define your vision statement, remember that it will reflect where you've been, where you are today, and what you think God wants to accomplish in your life in the future. That may look different in five or ten years, but in the meantime it can provide you with a long-term vantage point.

A vision statement is simply an expression of your life purpose.

For example, my vision statement, built off the Scripture verses from above, looks like this:

> I believe God has called me to be a servant of the gospel by the gift of His grace, given to me by the working of His power, and I believe that God has chosen me to share the good news, first with my family and friends, and then beyond, especially with women and the next generation, using the gifts and talents He's entrusted to my care.

You'll notice that my vision statement doesn't mention where I'd like to work or live, or even what I want to accomplish, although it touches upon what I am passionate about: God, my family, sharing the gospel, equipping women and the next generation. My vision doesn't mention how I'm going to do those things, because that's what goals do.

A vision statement is an identity statement that reminds you of who—and whose—you are.

What do you think your vision statement might look like? How can it reflect the story of your life and the ways the Word has been made real to you?

READY, SET, GOALS

While a vision statement lacks details, your goals describe the play-by-play for putting the dream or plan into action. Goals define how you want to fulfill your vision statement. They reflect your desires, which are influenced by your God-given wiring, passions, and circumstances.

By writing down your goals and taking time to reflect upon them later, you'll discover opportunities to praise God for the way He's been working in your life, even if it isn't how you expected.

Goals also provide a good reason to continue to seek God and watch for His work, even if His work is a rerouting of your goals! Unlike a vision statement, goals should be measurable in the following ways:

1. *Time.* What is the period of time in which each goal should be reached?

2. *Action.* Does each goal describe key steps, both ones that are realistic considering your resources as well as those which require trust in the Lord to see them accomplished?

3. *Result.* What evidence will indicate that you've met each goal?

For example, short- and long-term goals built from my vision statement may look like the following:

Short-Term Goal (one to three months): Over the next three months (time), I would like to share the gospel through continuing the habit of family devotions (action) and reading a Bible chapter each day after dinner (action) so that I can equip the children to consider ways to apply Scripture to their everyday lives (result).

Long-Term Goal (three to twelve months): Within the next year (time), I would like to get to know my neighbors by inviting them over for a meal or a cup of coffee (action), serving them in a time of need (action), and praying for them by name (action) so that they may feel the love of God through me (result) and come to know the Lord as their Savior in His perfect timing (result).

These are only two goals of many that I might have at a given time, depending upon the season of life. Of course, sometimes two is all I can handle! Regardless, they provide such a great way for me to check in with God and be intentional about how I'm living life. That's what I hope they'll do for you.

Goals provide a baseline for growth and give us something to work toward.

Your goals get to reflect your God-given wiring, experience, and life purpose. Writing them out may feel awkward at first, but if you push through the process, you'll experience the joy of connecting with God and seeing His hand in your life in the months to come.

READY, SET, GO

You've made it, my friend. Well done! You've reached the finish line of this journey! Do you feel elated? I hope so, because I want you to feel energized to keep on running forward, pressing toward the eternal finish line with a desire to glorify God each and every day! I pray that you will pursue this ongoing process of life transformation under the banner of God's grace, knowing that growth happens over time, one attitude shift and habit change at a time—and as you cultivate an authentic relationship with Christ and yield to His leading in every moment.

This may feel like the end of the race, but it's really just the beginning.

This is your starting line.

It's time to put into action all that you've learned! It's up to you to intentionally consider how your attitudes and habits are influencing the life you're living and the legacy you're leaving behind. So, friend, let me remind you:

Your thoughts influence your life. Will you take this challenge and commit to thinking about how you're living in light of God's Word?

When you own your thoughts, you own your habits, and then you can bring them before God and ask Him to change them . . . and change you. That's how you live a life for His glory as you become a part of His kingdom purposes. And in pursuing that vision, you'll find your purpose in becoming the new you—that woman God intended.

Trap and Transform

Cultivate Your Vision

It's time to summarize everything you've learned about yourself so that you can create a strong foundation for moving forward. The steps below will guide you in crafting a vision statement and goals.

Step 1: Summarize What You've Learned

Take your time answering these questions, reviewing your notes to see what stands out. Be intentionally prayerful in this process too.

1. *Relationships.* Whom do you believe God has called you to serve? Think in terms of people and the needs they have.

2. *Responsibilities.* What do you believe God has made you to do? Think in terms of skills, talents, and what you enjoy doing.

3. *Resources.* What do you believe God has made you the most passionate about? Think in terms of soapbox issues and causes you want to invest time and money in.

4. *Key Verse(s).* What Bible verses resonate with you the most? Are there any verses that capture the answers to the above questions?

Step 2: Craft a Vision Statement

Drawing from your answers to the questions above, craft a vision statement below. Use the key verse(s) to set up the framework for shaping the vision statement. If you feel stuck, flip back to my vision statement earlier in the chapter.

Based on _____ [verse], I believe that God has called me to _____ [relationships] by doing _____ [responsibilities] because I am passionate about _____ [resources].

Pray about what you have written. Fine-tune as needed. When you are ready, write out the final version of your vision statement:

Create a copy of your vision statement to keep in your Bible or in a frame on your desk, or even write it on your bathroom mirror using a whiteboard marker (not a permanent marker) so that you have a regular reminder of what God has done and is doing in your life. When it's time to make important decisions, especially in terms of relationships, responsibilities, and resources, pull out your vision statement to help discern what God is asking of you.

Step 3: Define Your Goals

Now it's time to write down your goals based on your vision statement. Make sure they are specific regarding time, action steps, and results. Think about your goals for a week or two before nailing them down, and when you feel a clear sense of direction, mark a date on the calendar for checking your progress.

Short-Term Goals (one to three months)

1.

2.

3.

Long-Term Goals (three to twelve months)

1.

2.

3.

If this process resonates with you, take some extra time to make long-term goals that stretch into years, such as one to two years, three to five years, and so on.

Step 4: Accountability and Checking In

Once you have your vision statement and goals nailed down, pick a date to do a check-in with the Lord. You might pick the first of every month or every quarter. Maybe you'll want to do it on your birth date every month. Set aside an hour to meet with the Lord as you look over your vision and goals. Evaluate what's worked and not worked. You might also want to do the life-mapping exercise again to see where you are. If by that you sense things are out of whack, complete a time-evaluation exercise in the following week as well as creating a new schedule with margin. Yes, all that you've done on this journey can become a part of your new mission to live intentionally!

Go Deeper

1. What is the number one, life-changing truth you've taken hold of during this journey?

2. What is one area you want to focus on in the next three months as a result of what you've discovered?

3. Imagine your life a year from now. What do you think will be the reward of living out the truths you've learned here?

Give It Over

Heavenly Father, may this moment be like a line drawn in the sand, marking my decision to press forward into ongoing transformative work. Help me to continue to cultivate fresh new attitudes and focused habits according to Your Word. Thank You, God, that You're the One who accomplishes Your work in me, for Your glory and good purposes. In Jesus's name, amen. (Proverbs 16:9; Philippians 3:12)

Afterword

Friend, it's been such an honor to lead you through this journey of meeting the new you. I'm praying for God's work to be evident to you, even today, as you wait until His full completion in eternity. I would love to continue to encourage you on this journey, so please join me at ElisaPulliam.com. You'll find complimentary resources that will encourage you in your faith and challenge you to continue this journey in meeting the new you.

Press on, sister. I'm certain that God has a great plan for using you to leave a radical impact on this world for His glory as He continues to make you into the woman He intended.

Acknowledgments

Writing this book would never have been possible if my husband had not challenged me to consider a life without Jesus. So thank you, Mr. Blue Eyes, for being the one who always saw the woman God intended me to become and for being my behind-the-scenes partner and advocate in life, parenting, ministry, and writing this book.

Leah, Abby, Luke, and Kaitlyn, thank you for your timely prayers, love-you-Momma hugs, and thoughtful questions. You have covered these writing days with such grace, which freed me to write about the truth we're building our lives upon. I love you kiddos. And Megan, I love you too! Your support has been like rich fuel to my soul.

Mom and Dad, your timely words of encouragement throughout this process spurred me on. Andrea, Michael, and Christopher, thank you for always being in my corner and making my life brighter. Dot, thank you for the significant way you shaped my understanding of the sovereignty of God. Bob, Katrina, Kim, and Mandy, thank you for supporting my writing from the very beginning.

My More to Be team, thank you for sharing in the mission of equipping moms, engaging teens, and encouraging mentors. In many ways, this book is the outcome of our co-laboring together. Prayer team and "mastermind" sisters, thank you for journeying through this process on your knees with me. Kingdom Hearts board, thank you for inspiring me to continue to embrace the story God is writing.

Emily and Marc, I am who I am today because of your influence, love, and prayers. Thank you for being a light in our lives! Susie R., until eternity I will thank God you were the one to show me Jesus in that London dorm room. Julie A., thank you for telling me to get God off my to-do list. Laura E., you might think you were only being a first-grade teacher, but you were really a life changer. Andrea R., thank you for calling me to seek God instead of pursuing His dreams for others. Stacie P., your love keeps me going—may we always consider ourselves sisters. Tonja D., you "knew me when" and continually spur me on to be who God intends—thank you!

Cara D., Martha P., and Marcia W., your faith-walks make mine grow and nurture my soul. Lucy S., thank you for supporting me at the most critical times! Cherie W. and Cheryl H., thank you for your love and mentorship. Jennifer C., if it wasn't for that last workshop at Allume . . . thank you! To my family at the Brook, I am so grateful for the part you've played in this journey.

Janet and Daryl Daughtry, I'm forever grateful for you and Life Breakthrough Coaching and Academy. Sue S., thank you for painting the most beautiful picture of how life coaching can change lives and for the impact you've had on mine!

Bill Jensen, thank you for entrusting me to the care of the very talented Ruth Samsel! Ruth, the way you've held my hand, waited for tears to dry, and trusted the outcome to the Lord with me is stunning. Thank you for not giving up, even when I doubted God's purposes.

Susan Tjaden and the whole team at WaterBrook Multnomah, thank you for bringing these words to life. Susan, your belief in this project from day one and your editorial expertise made this journey sweet for such a sensitive soul.

God, thank You for choosing me as Your own, long before I said yes to Your Son, Jesus Christ, as my Savior. I might have been crafting words since I was a little girl, but they found their purpose when I met You.

Notes

1. Kendra Cherry, "What Is Brain Plasticity?," About.com, http://psychology.about .com/od/biopsychology/f/brain-plasticity.htm.

2. Henry Blackaby, Richard Blackaby, and Claude King, *Experiencing God: Knowing and Doing the Will of God* (Nashville: Lifeway Church Resources, 1990), 14–15.

3. "Financial Peace University," DaveRamsey.com, www.daveramsey.com/fpu.

4. I heard James MacDonald teaching on this topic of trials and suffering during a weeklong family conference at Camp-of-the-Woods, Speculator, New York. You can learn more about Pastor MacDonald at http://jamesmacdonald.com and about this topic in his book *When Life Is Hard* (Chicago: Moody Publishers, 2010).

5. Dee Brestin, *The God of All Comfort: Finding Your Way into His Arms* (Grand Rapids, MI: Zondervan, 2009), 190.

6. Karen Ehman, *Let It Go: How to Stop Running the Show and Start Walking in Faith* (Grand Rapids, MI: Zondervan, 2012), 156.

7. Marita Littauer and Florence Littauer, *Wired That Way Companion Workbook: A Comprehensive Guide to Understanding and Maximizing Your Personality Type* (Ventura, CA: Regal Books, 2006).

8. "Our Theory," 16Personalities.com, www.16personalities.com/articles/our-theory.

9. "Why MBTI," MBTI, www.mbtionline.com.

10. William Moulton Marston, *Emotions of Normal People* (Louth, UK: Cooper, 2014), 174–75.

11. "Strengths," http://strengths.gallup.com/default.aspx.

12. This test requires a fee associated with working with a Highlands consultant. To learn more about this assessment, visit www.highlandsco.com or www .elisapulliam.com/life-coaching/services.

13. Priscilla Shirer, *Gideon: Your Weakness. God's Strength* (Nashville: LifeWay Church Resources, 2013), 70.

14. We will be talking about talents, spiritual gifts, calling, and passion over the next few days. For the sake of clarity, allow me to differentiate them: *talent*— something you simply enjoy doing but doesn't reflect a cause or have a significant purpose (according to the world's standards); *spiritual gift*—given by God for the building up and equipping of the body of Christ; *calling*—what you feel

you were created to do (sometimes also your career); *passion*—something you are bent on doing because of your life experience and/or wiring, or a cause you want to devote time to.

15. Logos 6 Bible Software, *Hebrew-Aramaic Dictionary of the New American Standard Exhaustive Concordance* (La Habra, CA: The Lockman Foundation, 1998).

16. Deb Peterson, "Learning Styles—The Controversy," About.com, http://adulted .about.com/od/Learning-Styles/tp/Learning-Styles-The-Controversy.htm.

17. If you want to further explore learning styles, especially as they relate to education, career, and ministry choices, consider the Highlands Ability Battery at www.highlandsco.com.

18. "Number of Jobs Held, Labor Market Activity, and Earnings Growth Among the Youngest Baby Boomers: Results from a Longitudinal Survey," July 25, 2012, Bureau of Labor Statistics, US Department of Labor, USDL 12-1489, www .bls.gov/news.release/archives/nlsoy_07252012.pdf, 1.

19. "Three Trends on Faith, Work, and Family," Barna Group, February 11, 2014, www.barna.org/barna-update/culture/649-three-major-faith-and-culture-trends -for-2014#.VP7olUaemSU.

20. "Serving God in Our Culture," Focus on the Family, www.focusonthefamily .com/media/daily-broadcast/serving-god-in-our-culture.

21. "Barna Survey Examines Changes in Worldview Among Christians over the Past 13 Years," Barna Group, March 6, 2009, www.barna.org/barna-update /21-transformation/252-barna-survey-examines-changes-in-worldview-among- christians-over-the-past-13-years#.VIhuvlt0yyI.

22. Larry Osborne, *Ten Dumb Things Smart Christians Believe: Are Urban Legends and Sunday School Myths Damaging Your Faith?* (Colorado Springs, CO: Multnomah, 2009), 4.

23. Osborne, *Ten Dumb Things Smart Christians Believe,* 6.

24. If you would like to learn more about idolatry and its manifestations in your life, I highly recommend you to Brad Bigney's series at https://bradbigney.wordpress .com/2013/04/02/230 and to make full use of his resources found online at https://bradbigney.wordpress.com/idols-of-the-heart-2.

25. Sarah Young, *Jesus Calling* (Nashville: Thomas Nelson, 2010), December 11.

26. Brad Bigney, *Gospel Treason* (Phillipsburg, NJ: P&R Publishing, 2012), 20.

27. Bigney, *Gospel Treason,* 21.

28. R. T. Kendall, *Total Forgiveness* (Lake Mary, FL: Charisma House, 2002), 90.

29. Kendall, *Total Forgiveness,* 14.

30. "The Scruggs," IAmSecond.com, www.iamsecond.com/seconds/the-scruggs.

31. Beth Moore, *Children of the Day: 1 and 2 Thessalonians* (Nashville: LifeWay Press, 2014), 24.

32. Marshal Segal, "A Song for the Suffering (with John Piper)," *desiringGod* (blog), August 13, 2013, www.desiringgod.org/blog/posts/a-song-for-the-suffering -with-john-piper.

33. Jennifer Dukes Lee, *Love Idol: Letting Go of Your Need for Approval—and Seeing Yourself Through God's Eyes* (Carol Stream, IL: Tyndale Momentum, 2014), 120.

34. Richard A. Swenson, *Margin: Restoring Emotional, Physical, Financial, and Time Reserves to Overloaded Lives* (Colorado Springs, CO: NavPress, 2004), 13, 15.

35. Meet Tsh Oxenreider at http://tshoxenreider.com and http://theartofsimple.net.

36. Anne Ortlund, *The Gentle Ways of the Beautiful Woman: A Practical Guide to Spiritual Beauty* (Edison, NJ: Inspirational, 1998), 96.

37. Dave Ramsey, *Dave Ramsey's Complete Guide to Money* (Brentwood, TN: Lampo, 2011), 141–42.